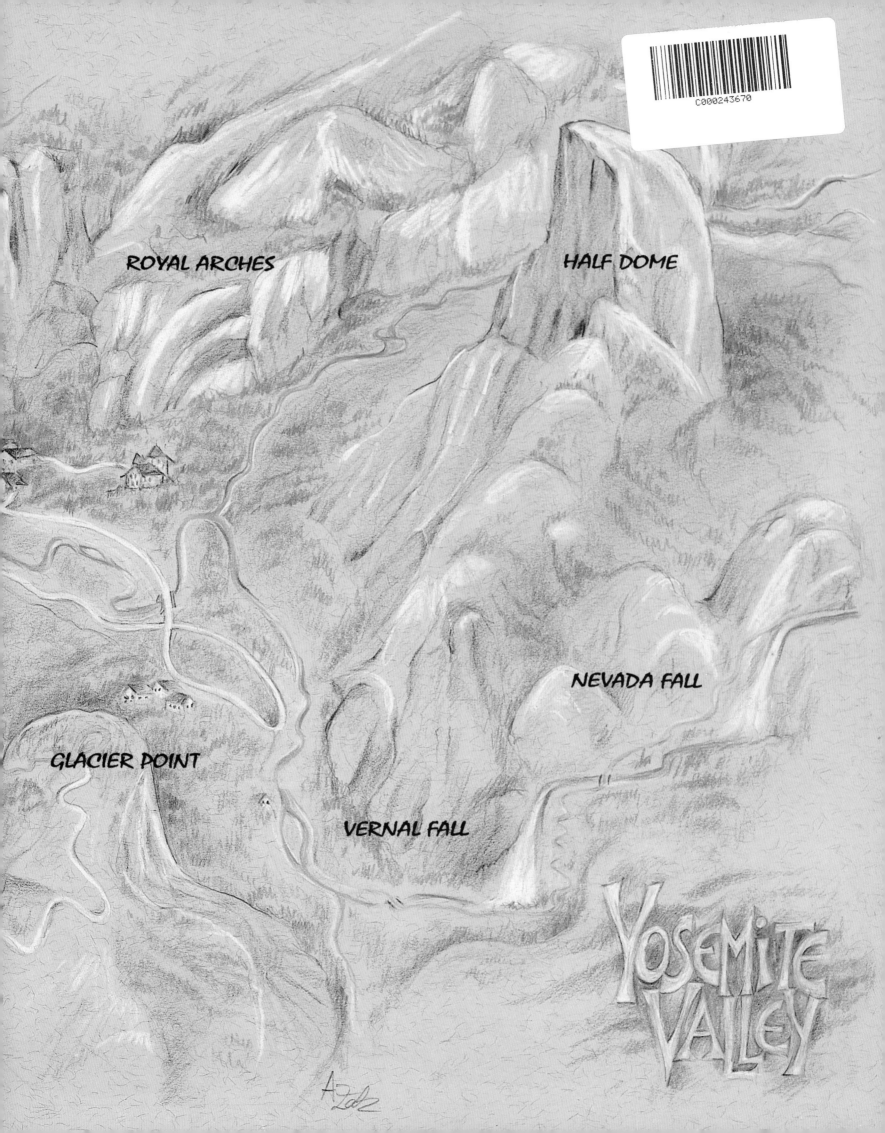

ROYAL ARCHES

HALF DOME

NEVADA FALL

GLACIER POINT

VERNAL FALL

YOSEMITE VALLEY

YOSEMITE

Half a Century of Dynamic Rock Climbing

Alexander Huber
Heinz Zak

Half a Century of Dynamic Rock Climbing

photographs by Heinz Zak
text by Alexander Huber

with special contributions from:
Jim Bridwell, Mark Chapman, Peter Croft,
Warren Harding, Lynn Hill, Leo Houlding,
Thomas Huber, John Long, Jerry Moffatt,
Dean Potter, Royal Robbins, and Heinz Zak.

Adapted from a translation by Nadya Stracey

Menasha Ridge Press
Birmingham, Alabama. U.S.A.

Bâton Wicks
London. U.K.

Trade enquiries in the UK and the Commonwealth (except Canada) to:
Cordee, 3a De Montfort Street, Leicester LE1 7HD
Trade enquiries in the USA and Canada to:
The Globe Pequot Press, P.O.Box 480, Guilford, CT 06437, Tel. (800) 243-0495

British Library Cataloguing in Publication Data:
A catalogue record for this book exists at the British Library ISBN 1-898573-57-3 (UK)
Library of Congress Cataloging in Publication Data:
A catalog record of this book exists at the Library of Congress ISBN 0-89732-557-5 (USA)

ACKNOWLEDGEMENTS Thanks are due to Royal Robbins, Jim Bridwell, John Long, Mark Chapman, Jerry Moffatt, Peter Croft, Dean Potter, Lynn Hill, Thomas Huber, Leo Houlding and the late Warren Harding for their contributions to the book. Linda McMillan of the American Alpine Club and Tom Frost were generous with research assistance and advice. Birgit König edited the text and Angelika Zak designed the book. The English language text was adapted from a translation by Nadya Stracey (bulk of the text) with additional work by Gill Round, Gabriela Oates and Chris Fitzhugh.

Throughout the book we have quoted words attributed to famous climbers first put in print in the books, journals and magazines listed below, often as a result of original research. In this respect we would particularly like to thank Steve Roper, not only for the inspiration and guidance we gained from his book *Camp 4* but also for his guidance in preparing the English language edition and navigating a way through a range of unexpected editorial problems. In a similar manner we are also indebted to Gary Arce for the guidance given by his later history and also pay tribute to the late Galen Rowell, George Meyers, the late Reinhard Karl and Pat Ament for the inspiration, gained from their books on Yosemite. For additional photographs we wish to thank: Tom Frost – 37 (lower), 42, 50, 56, 61, 63 and 65; Wayne Merry – 45; Christian Gabl – 16; the estate of Wolfgang Güllich – 79; Peter Janschek – 2, 17, 18 (upper) and 93; John Long archive – 108; the late Galen Rowell 44, 59; Bill Westbay archive – 106; Angelika Zak – 13 (right); Ian Parnell – 169. Thanks are also due to the many climbers who have assisted us in getting photographs of the key pitches of some very inaccessible climbs.

The following books, journals and magazines have been consulted during the preparation of this history: *The Vertical World of Yosemite* (1) by Galen Rowell (California, 1974); *Yosemite Climber* (2) by George Meyers (London and Modesto, 1979); *Yosemite* (3) by Reinhard Karl (Bad Homberg, 1982); *Camp 4* (4) by Steve Roper (Seattle and London, 1994). *Defying Gravity* (5) by Gary Arce (Berkeley, 1996); *Royal Robbins – Spirit of the Age* (6) by Pat Ament (Mechanicsburg, 1998). *The American Alpine Journal* (7), and the magazines *Climbing* (8) and *Rock and Ice* (9) have also been sources of information. The numbers in parentheses are used throughout the text to indicate the source of quotations, additional sources being noted by asterisk*. Another special form used later in the book is that for indicating aid-climbing grades – the original grade is given first and, where suitable, the modern grade follows: thus North America Wall is graded (A5/5.8 now A3/5.8). The author's natural metric height and distance terminology is maintained but imperial measurements are retained in the invited essays and historic quotations as seems most suitable for their source. Editor's footnotes are sometimes added giving extra detail about an incident or controversy.

4

CONTENTS

All uncredited chapters are written by Alexander Huber

Left: The view to Half Dome from Glacier Point

Page 1: The Lightning Bolt symbol on Columbia Boulder

Page 2: Heinz Zak attempting High Heaven (5.12d) on Glacier Point

Page 6: Cedar Wright on Tips (5.12a), one of Yosemite's best finger crack climbs

Page 7: Randy Leavitt on his route Book of Hate (5.13d), Elephant's Graveyard

Below: Randy Leavitt and a large piece of gear on Bad Ass Momma (5.11d). Right and far right: Airlie Anderson on Fish Crack (5.12b), Cascade Falls

Below right: Steph Davis on Tales of Power (5.12b)

Left: Hall of Mirrors (5.12d) on Glacier Point Apron. Since a huge rock slide great care is required when climbing here.

Below left: Wolfgang Güllich on Electric Africa (5.12c), Tuolumne

Below right: Heinz Zak on Blues Riff (5.11c), Tuolumne

Page 11: To the background of the thundering waters of Yosemite Falls Bernhard Hangl makes progress on Freestone (5.11c)

Page 11: Alex Huber sport climbing on Taft Point with the lower half of The Nose in the background

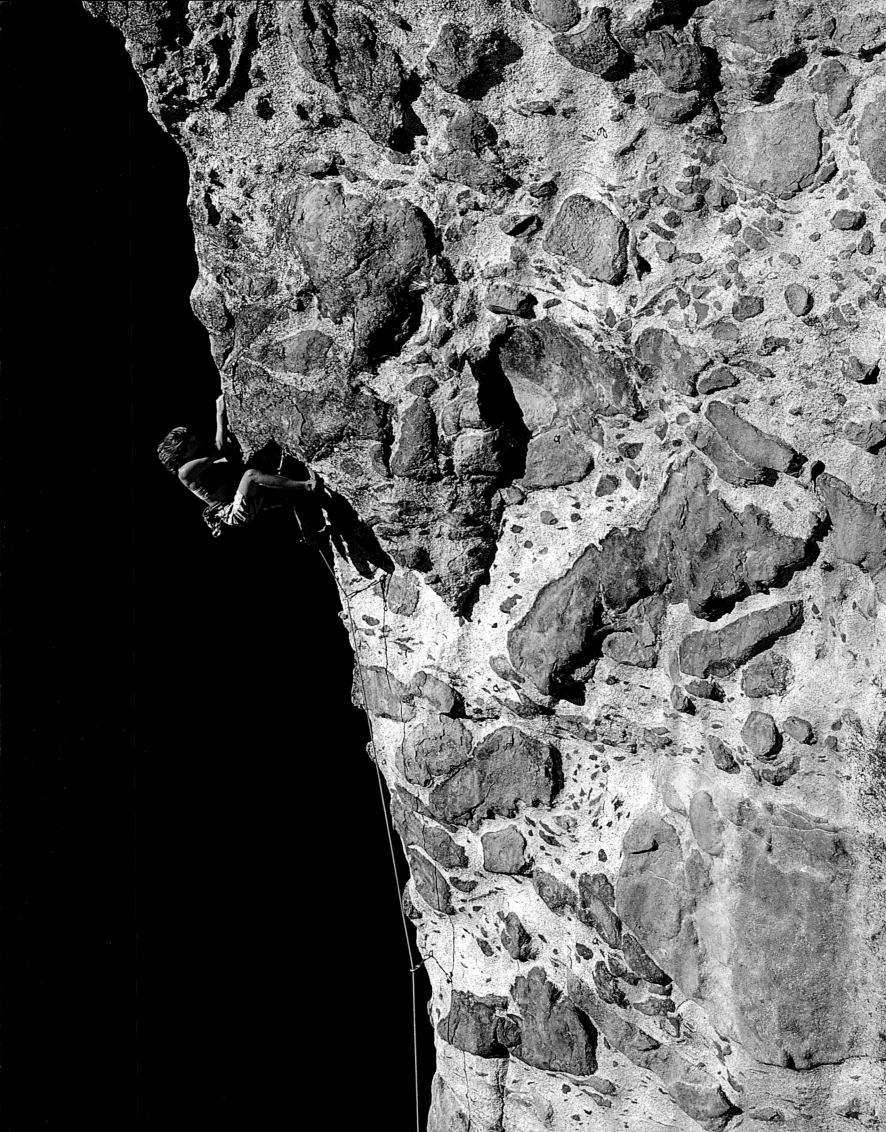

Opposite page: Blanka Kantorova on the impressive Killer Pillar, Elephant Rock

Left: The lower slabs of Nutcracker (5.8), Manure Pile Buttress

Lower left: The third pitch of the East Buttress (5.10a) of El Capitan

Below: A team on Serenity Cracks (5.10d), Royal Arches

Heinz Zak

FOREWORD

'Never, absolutely never, will I be able to climb this pig of a crack!' I am hanging on the rope, exhausted, gasping for breath, after only two of the forty metres. 'It cannot be possible' is the thought that lurked.

Pushing aside defeatism I re-enter the monster. Jamming my elbow on the left, with my right hand I build up so much pressure at the edge of the crack that I can free my wedged foot and jam it ten centimetres higher and then repeat the process. After five metres of this I've finally had enough. Both knuckles are bleeding and my elbow and left knee are hurting. The hope of making a free ascent of Free Rider finally seems to be disappearing. How am I supposed to lead this forty metre offwidth if I can't even manage a few metres on a top rope? Peter and I don't give up. We tape our knuckles and bandage elbows and knees.

Three weeks later we are on our way. I push our only No.6 Friend in front of me as questionable protection. I don't want to think about the possibility of a mega fall. I puff and groan in the most awful juice extractor in the world! Even staying in the crack requires energy – how I would love to let go in order to finally be free of the exertions. But it must be simple. This crack, graded 5.11b, is harder for me than the following 5.12d rope lengths! Persistence and motivation give me the strength – three days later the free ascent is behind us.

Like no other climbing area, Yosemite routes leave deep memories that anchor my heart firmly to this magical valley. The constant sunshine in the steel blue sky, the thundering waterfalls, the turquoise-green stream, the fantastic way of life in the dust of Camp 4 or the enjoyable hours in El Cap Meadow and the Mountain Room Bar – all of this fills me again with the longing to go back and visit this special place with all its climbers. Chongo, the man who knows how to enjoy life, Dean Potter the solo climber and master of the slackline, Platinum Rob Miller – likeable and always friendly, Jay Selvidge (the laundry man), Ammon McNeely the techno freak and the speed climber Cedar Wright. Or the ever-successful Jim Bridwell, Tom Frost, Jo Whitford and Chelsea Griffie – they have all unbelievably enriched my life. So strong were these impressions that I had the desire to capture it all on the camera long before I eventually learned to take a proper photograph.

The first time my knees were knocking was in 1979. After an ascent of East Buttress on El Capitan I had spent the night on the summit because I wanted to watch a group of skydivers the next morning as they made their daring jump over the 1000m high wall. By chance I was offered the role of photographer. Totally inexperienced in challenging action photography I belayed myself to the precipice. Standing right on the edge I waited for the jump. The tense atmosphere of the group was electrifying and I suddenly felt like one of the players. An experienced base jumper was directing the group. He gave good advice and in the very last seconds controlled the countdown of the jumper: 'Step forward to the edge, move back three feet. Three, two, one, go!' My heart starts beating fast still today when I think of that first jump – then my heart was drumming against my ribcage and as the first person jumped my knees began to knock involuntarily so that I had to sit down straight away.

In the last twenty-three years I have had many chances as a photographer to be present at such hair-raising and climbing and jumping activities. I experienced my most exciting moments with Wolfgang Güllich on

11 October 1986. It was a cool morning in the Valley. A light breeze was playing around the edge of the six-metre roof crack Separate Reality and the sun, which was shining on the granite slab below, turned the often bleak and gloomy looking roof a golden yellow. Everything was quiet. The Merced river was glistening far below, but neither the sound of it or the noise of the traffic rose up to us from below. We only exchanged a few words. Wolfgang's hands were shaking when he smeared chalk on the back of his hands. He kept dipping his hand into his chalk bag,

to let time stand still perhaps or to bide his time for the moment when his spirit gave the OK for the solo ascent. I hung below the roof without moving. I was choked with nervousness.

I couldn't hide the shaking in my voice and in my body. I wanted be there and at the same time didn't want to – the idea that Wolfgang's jams could slip out of the crack and he would fall to certain death was hammering inside my skull. Equally, the burden of my possible failure as a photographer on this unique and, to this day, unparalleled ascent tormented me. This had been the reason for my travelling to Yosemite on this occasion. Wolfgang had already let me into his amazingly daring plan some months previously. And so the time had come. Suddenly everything seemed to go so quickly. Squarely and unsteadily Wolfgang climbed the first few metres up to me, his body trembling with tension and excitement. After the first few metres in the roof all the nervousness appeared to fall away. Through the viewfinder I watched Wolfgang Güllich in his metier as a precise climbing machine, every movement considered and thought through and confidently executed right to the end. With a loud cry never heard from him before, he trumpeted his relief and joy as he eventually gained the lip of the roof.

I have become a full-time professional climbing photographer since 1985, abseiling down climbs to reach ideal camera positions, often with complicated rope manoeuvres. Of particular note was the trip down to the enormous headwall of the Salathé Wall in May 1995 which introduced me to a new and unusual photographic dimension. Days beforehand I had belayed Alexander Huber on the first redpoint ascent of this great climb. We now abseiled from above to take photographs. An uneasy feeling crept over me. The featureless face plummeted down 900m

Right: Heinz Zak on Separate Reality (5.11d)

Below: Base jumping from El Capitan

below me. The yawning emptiness below my feet at first rather depressed my spirits. It took time to get used to the great exposure and slowly I dared to make the otherwise unfamiliar rope manoeuvres. In the end this experience was so challenging that I asked Alexander for a second photo shoot as I was simply not sure if I had covered everything properly. The second session again lasted two days and resulted in better pictures! I had fixed the rope eighty metres above me and it was hanging free. For hours I swung to and fro in the wind, spun around and jumared up and down to change position while Alexander repeatedly climbed the most difficult sections. His dedication spurred me on to produce the best results. It was a great success – the pictures appeared in many of the world's climbing magazines!

Since then I have kept returning to El Capitan. The fear has given way to enthusiasm. For me there is nothing better than to photograph the world's best climbers on this huge rock face. The unbelievable dimension, the enormous lines on a constantly glistening sea of granite continue to fascinate me.

In the last few years I have also photographed totally crazy activities in Yosemite – Dean Potter ropeless on the North-West Face of Half Dome and slack-lining with protection on Lost Arrow and unprotected on the Rostrum. Meanwhile I have become calmer as a photographer helped by my complete trust in the climbers with whom I am working. I have been privileged to witness so many amazing events and it has also been very enjoyable working with all the Valley climbers who are now immortalised in this book. To all of them I offer my heartfelt thanks for their willing help and friendly support and I hope that climbers who acquire this book will be correspondingly inspired to visit and climb in this extraordinary place.

1 YOSEMITE

Monolithic granite walls and thundering waterfalls – these are the attractions for tourist masses who pour into Yosemite National Park every year. The famous American naturalist John Muir described Yosemite Valley as the 'incomparable valley', which constitutes only a tiny part of the 3100-square-kilometre national park in the Californian Sierra Nevada. From the scores of 4000m barren rocky peaks of the High Sierra the park extends down to the forests and river meadows of the deeply cut Yosemite Valley. Impressive rock bastions like Half Dome and El Capitan sitting majestically above the Valley, interspersed with fabulous waterfalls, have drawn attention to Yosemite as an incomparable spectacle of nature. For some of the visitors to the Valley these vertical rock deserts promise added adventure as this unique collection of dramatic granite walls and spires forms a Mecca for international climbers.

From the moment you enter the Valley on one of its three access roads you will be overwhelmed. You will be captivated by the scenery and amazed by the stupendous rock architecture as you look across all of these famous cliffs. For climbers, peaks and precipices of Yosemite are not merely a backdrop – for them the rocks and cliffs resonate with the potential for challenge and adventure. This vertical world was and is the scene of many a gripping story – great successes as well as moving human dramas. The names of the pioneers are immortalised in the granite of the Valley and much climbing history was written here. Many articles and books about the great days in the mountains have been published to be eagerly devoured by climbers, adventuring in their imaginations before they finally experience the 'incomparable valley' for the first time.*

At the age of fourteen, I was given Reinhard Karl's book *Time to Breathe*. It wasn't long before I had read all his books. I was fascinated by the world he described and I dreamt of being in the mountains myself – the Alps, the Himalaya, Patagonia and Yosemite. Long before I was to make my first visit to the Valley I was already there in spirit and had already climbed many of these big mountains in my head. But for the present they were only dreams – the inexhaustible challenges in the Alps were too close and the mountains of the world were too far away – even Yosemite.

My dream became reality in 1995: I set off to Yosemite because of the big walls, some of the most difficult and highest in the world. In April I was finally standing in awe in the dust of the legendary Camp 4. I wasn't disappointed. Though I looked in vain for the heroes, I did find something of Yosemite's famous past. Climbers from all over the world meet today on this fabled campground. Although the earlier community of the 'residents' who lived in the camp for whole seasons no longer exists, the visiting climbers still form a bonded community. The meeting point remains the Columbia Boulder in the centre of the campground where you can be sure of an audience during an ascent of the famous boulder problem – Midnight Lightning.

Yet the climbing in Yosemite is quite varied – the Valley has a generous supply of routes to suit every taste. However, the majority of non-local climbers are attracted by the big walls – the embodiment of Yosemite climbing. More than forty years ago big wall techniques were developed here and since then these vertiginous cliffs have lost nothing of their fascination. To 'do' a big wall means to opt out of normal life for days. There is only one aim and that's the summit – the more difficulties that present themselves on the way, the more lasting the memory.

El Capitan reflected in the Merced River

The Valley is also the perfect place to recover from such profound exertions. Climbing intensity and desire is balanced by cafeteria, bar, pizzeria or a dip in the Merced river. Other natural attractions also offer balm. A walk up to Vernal and Nevada Falls, a hike over the fascinating landscape of the Valley rim or a detour to Tuolumne Meadows – all serve to clear the head and refocus one's ambitions. The cycle of recovery is thus completed and the game of 'climbing' begins all over again.

*I am indebted to Steve Roper for his book *Camp 4* which I have used as a source for many of the stories and incidents described in the early chapters of this book. He was there during the early days of Yosemite climbing, both as an eye-witness and a participant and he also compiled the first major guidebook to the area.

Yosemite Valley from the Tunnel View

Far Left: Rainbow in the spray of the Vernal Fall

Left: Jeffrey Pine on Sentinel Dome

Below: El Cap Tree

25

Half Dome from Olmsted Point, Tuolumne

2 Exploring the Sierra Nevada

Long before the first white people landed in America, Yosemite Valley was inhabited by native Americans. The steep faces which sealed off the Valley on all sides gave the Ahwahneechee, a subtribe of the Sierra Miwok, protection from intruders. Sheltered from the raw climate of the higher Sierra Nevada, the luxuriant nature of the Valley offered a sustainable living. On the site of today's Yosemite Village there used to be a settlement of permanent tents. The Ahwahneechee not only roamed the Valley as hunters, they also travelled across the surrounding mountains, and it is likely that they climbed many accessible peaks.

Life changed for the Ahwahneechee with the arrival of white people. At the beginning of the nineteenth century the first groups wandered through the High Sierra, and in 1833 they stood in front of the breathtaking view from the rim of the 900m-deep Valley – white people had discovered Yosemite.

The original inhabitants of the Valley had only a few years left. Gold was discovered at the foot of the Sierra Nevada. Streams of fortune hunters followed the gold rush to California and even the remotest regions were penetrated. Within a few years unspoiled countryside was transformed into a battleground and the Ahwahneechee, settlers and gold-diggers found themselves in competition. The Ahwahneechee defended their homeland with more and more determination. But the settlers and gold-seekers organised themselves and sent a punitive expedition into Yosemite in 1851. The Ahwahneechee were captured and deported. Though they were allowed to return briefly, Yosemite Valley was by then lost as their homeland. Things calmed down for a period and people took no notice of the Valley thanks to its isolated position. In those days life on the western frontier was so tough that most settlers would have been far too preoccupied with the problems of living to take time to visit the sights of Yosemite.

Yosemite was surveyed in 1863 when geologists first explored the Sierra Nevada. To get an overview of the landscape the group led by Josiah Whitney climbed onto the plateau and continued north to the prominent vantage point of Mount Hoffmann, the first of many peaks that they were to climb during the survey. The snow-covered chain of the High Sierra was in the east, the granite domes towered above the forests of Tuolumne Meadows to the north and in the south they saw the striking silhouette of Half Dome.

Alpine climbing was already established in Europe with ambitious members of the Alpine Club vying for the first ascents of the most difficult summits. In the Sierra Nevada climbing was still primarily on the more easily accessible and prominent peaks. Nevertheless this was an important step for the future development of mountaineering in the Sierra Nevada. The ascent of the highest points was soon to be seen no longer for purely surveying reasons and it became the geologists' passion.

> 'Such a landscape!' enthused William Brewer. 'A hundred peaks in sight of over 13,000ft, deep canyons, cliffs in every direction, sharp ridges almost inaccessible to man on which the human foot has never trod – all combined to produce a view which few are privileged to behold.'

On the occasion of the first ascent of Mount Brewer that was named after their leader, the geologists noted a peak sixty miles to the south that appeared to be the highest in the Sierra Nevada. This they named Mount

Whitney in honour of the leader of their group. One of the explorers, the young Clarence King, was not only thrilled by the view but was also fired by the idea of being the first human to ascend the peak. Only a few days later he started out with a colleague. The advance on Mount Whitney was then still thought of as an expedition. Over a stretch of thirty miles the two of them crossed deep gorges, enormous forests, high mountain chains and had already been on their way for two days before they reached the foot of their destination. After a cold open bivouac they climbed up across easy slopes to the summit ridge and were soon standing on the highest point. A triumphant moment – but unfortunately they were standing on the summit of the wrong mountain. Without a map they had not realised their mistake until they had reached the summit where they saw Mount Whitney a few miles further to the south!

King did not admit defeat and during the next ten years he made repeated attempts but was unsuccessful each time. On another occasion he again found himself standing on the wrong peak, Mount Langley, finding a cairn with an arrow on the summit. This time he could see the object of his desire just a short distance to the north. Despite all his efforts, the struggle to make the first ascent of this highest mountain of the Sierra Nevada ended for King in 1873 – Charles Begole, Albert Johnson and John Lucas, three fishermen from the Owens Valley, reached the coveted summit (14,494ft) before him.

With the measuring of the Sierra Nevada, Yosemite Valley's unique character had been identified. A group of influential citizens advocated the protection of the Valley and in 1864 Yosemite Valley became a State Park, the first protected park in America. The Valley was given over to the management of the State of California with the directive that the landscape should be kept in its original state and made accessible to the public. At that time the State Park covered a comparatively small area: only the deeply cut valley itself and the Mariposa Grove at the entrance to the Valley with the gigantic Sequoias were included. Soon afterwards a young Scottish immigrant was to have a decisive influence on its future development: in the spring of 1868 John Muir landed in the port of San Francisco having heard rumours of an incomparably beautiful valley of waterfalls and mountains in the Sierra Nevada. Muir was captivated by Yosemite. At a time when America was still devastated by the Civil War and the West was still 'wild', Muir's interest in nature and geology was in advance of its time. His enthusiasm and his open eye for all aspects of the environment were unique at a time when much in life was still taken for granted. Like no one else in his era he saw 'a glorious array of white peaks, deep in the sky, every feature glowing, radiating beauty'.

John Muir was to become one of the most important naturalists in America. He was not only an admirer and chronicler of nature but also a riveting story-teller and author. His gift was of being at home in nature, of experiencing it, and then extolling and conveying its beauties, Muir thus came to be the ambassador of Yosemite. Twenty-five years after the creation of the State Park he asserted his influence in the founding of the Yosemite National Park that extended from the Valley bottom up to the highest summits of the Sierra Nevada, thereby encompassing the whole of the eco-system of Yosemite with its mountains, forests, rivers, plateaus and valleys. In 1890 after many campaigning articles John Muir's wish came to fruition and Yosemite National Park was established as the second oldest national park in the world after Yellowstone. In order to lend more weight to his ideas Muir also founded the Sierra Club in 1892 (notables and mountaineers) to promote understanding of nature and safeguard its originality.

Many mountaineers from the Sierra Club took up the fight for the preservation of the wilderness. David Brower, for example, was one of the best and most motivated climbers of the 1930s. Over many years he spent the summer months in the High Sierra and later became a key figure in the environmental movement. He produced the first colour films of the High Sierra, won recognition with publications and lectures and awakened an interest in the respectful treatment of the environment in wide-reaching sections of the population. Following in the tradition of Muir, his work also enjoyed political success as he played a part in the establishment of no less than five national parks and many other protected areas.

3 Early Yosemite Climbers

After the highest summits of the High Sierra had been climbed via their easiest routes, the few climbers around at that time began to look for further challenges. There were still numbers of unclimbed peaks that were technically difficult and often described as 'impossible'. One early climbing pioneer was John Muir. His first ascent of the forbidding Cathedral Peak in 1869 involved sustained rock scrambling and Class 4 rock climbing on the final section to the summit. 'I never weary gazing at the wonderful Cathedral' wrote Muir, 'it has more individual character than any other rock or mountain I ever saw excepting perhaps the Yosemite South Dome.'*

Another noteworthy event of the period was the spectacular and controversial first ascent of Half Dome. In 1875, after many had already failed on the compact slabs of its summit structure, George Anderson, the Yosemite blacksmith, tackled the problem using primitive aid techniques. He brought specially forged iron stakes with eyes that he hammered into bored holes. From one borehole to the next he worked his way up the slabby face making slow but secure progress. Showing great stamina and determination after over a hundred holes and stakes he completed this remarkable route. He hoped to open it as an early *via ferrata* and charge tourists for the ascent, but this idea, and his methods, were controversial and were criticised by Muir and others. Even before climbing could be defined as a mountain sport, the debate had started about the excessive use of bolts.

After this unconventional ascent the development that followed luckily took a more sporting path. Those active in the Sierra Club were, above all, mountaineers who moved safely and fast on alpine rock, and they steadily mastered the rock peaks of the

High Sierra. But they were not climbers versed in the more technical skills that would soon be needed. While in the Alps big walls were being tackled in the early 1900s, Yosemite climbing remained isolated and backward. Progress in technical climbing was not made until 1931. Francis Farquhar, the publisher of the *Sierra Club Bulletin*, had climbed with former fellow students from Harvard in British Columbia in the summer of 1930. Amongst them was Robert Underhill who, as a result of his successes in the Mont Blanc massif and later on the Grand Teton, had become an international climber of high reputation. Underhill convinced his companions to use European climbing methods, and in February 1931 his knowledge of the use and management of the rope was published in the Bulletin. It wasn't long before climbers of the Sierra Club were to be found searching for new objectives.

These highly motivated climbers didn't have long to wait for success. Together with their mentor Underhill, Norman Clyde and the students Jules Eichorn and Glen Dawson made the first ascent of the East Face of Mount Whitney (5.4) in the summer of 1931.

During the following winter Eichorn began to train with Dick Leonard, Bestor Robinson and others. On small rock outcrops in Berkeley they developed the skills of secure belaying and competent abseiling. This went as far as testing their belaying by taking trial falls off overhangs to be held by fellow climbers. Through trial and error, they determined that the waist belay coupled with a dynamic (sliding) arrest was the most effective method of holding a falling climber and avoiding the hemp rope breaking. It was this thorough training that gave them the confidence for their early Yosemite explorations.

By the 1930s all the big peaks of the High Sierra had been climbed. However, an enormous field of activity

* From *My First Summer in the Sierra* (Boston, 1911).

now opened up with the new techniques, the most obvious challenges being Yosemite's dramatic walls and the granite needles.

In the summer of 1933 the trio turned their attention to the Cathedral Spires – two rock towers which rose 200m into the sky, like rockets out of the forest – seemingly vertical, smooth and 'impossible'.

Their first attempt on the South Face of Higher Cathedral Spire came to naught. After four hours of unsuccessful struggling on its South-West Face and another three hours on the East Face they were defeated by difficulties that were too great for their primitive equipment. Their pitons were nothing more than long nails! But they didn't give up. In November they returned equipped with modern pitons and karabiners bought from the Sporthaus Schuster in Munich. They managed two rope lengths of difficult climbing before darkness forced them to turn back again. Another winter passed, during which they acquired more pitons and studied photos of the

Spire trying to discern the best line to attack. In April 1934, aided by the pitons they had already placed, they renewed their attempt. Robinson and Leonard took turns leading. At the hardest point Leonard found a traverse left to turn the difficulties. They then made progress to the final crack where they resorted to their pitons to gain the summit of Higher Cathedral Spire (A1/5.5 now 5.8) just as the sun was setting.

A few months later the same team managed the first ascent of the Lower Cathedral Spire (A1/5.6 now 5.9). Both ascents demanded technical advances that were new for Yosemite climbers. Although twin rope technique, aid climbing and pendulum traverses had been used in Europe for twenty years they were innovative steps for American climbing. The Cathedral Spires saga might thus be regarded as the first important rock-climbing event in Yosemite Valley.

After that, first ascents were more numerous and visits to Yosemite by climbers became more frequent. Their meeting point was then Camp 9 near the Ahwahnee Hotel but it was still a fairly small community that came together here to prepare for the next trips into the wilderness.

'It was marvellous to be a climber back then. Everybody knew everybody else very well. There was no competition, probably because we weren't smart enough to be competitive! No egos got in the way or had to be massaged. We were just a bunch of really good friends. I remember a lot of days when we weren't necessarily climbing, but just out exploring the Valley. We enjoyed a lot of lovely days, far from tourists, not doing anything particularly difficult, but just enjoying each other's company. We were very much a family.'

Royal Arches

Below: Jo Whitford soloing the "Regular" route (now free at 5.9) on Royal Arches

Morgan Harris's simple love of Valley life is apparent from this account. Like many others in the 'family' he had little money. The 300km journey from San Francisco by bike was standard practice! Climbing was pursued in a more committed fashion, first ascents were sought and the big, still unclimbed, walls were probed for possible routes of ascent. One challenge close at hand was the enormous granite curve of Royal Arches that formed a breathtaking backdrop directly above the Ahwahnee Hotel. After two unsuccessful attempts, Harris successfully climbed it in October 1936 together with Ken Adam and Kenneth Davis (A1/5.6 now 5.9). Like the first ascent of Cathedral Spires this wall also demanded new ideas. Failure served as the motivation to refine techniques and equipment until eventually an attempt would be crowned with success.

4 Salathé's Climbs

After the ascents of Cathedral Spires and Royal Arches Yosemite climbers would have been ready for more difficult objectives, but the time was not yet right: on 7 December 1941 the Japanese bombed the American Pacific Fleet in Pearl Harbor and until the end of World War II, the focus of the United States was on world events. The unimportant things in life were pushed to one side and there was little or no climbing in Yosemite during this time.

With the end of hostilities everything changed. There was no longer a lack of climbing gear as ex-military ropes, pitons and lightweight karabiners were plentiful. Climbers came back full of motivation and a few of them were thinking about the three obvious problems: Lost Arrow Spire, the South-West Face of Half Dome and the North Face of Sentinel Rock.

Lost Arrow Spire was already special to the Ahwahneechees. They thought that the gods had created this slender needle as a memorial to the hunter Kos-soo-kah. According to folklore he fell down the wall as he attempted to send a message with an arrow into the Valley to his beloved.

In 1935 Dick Leonard had already shown interest in this tower which is split off from the enormous granite wall on the right of Yosemite Falls. He embarked on the first attempt when he abseiled down from the Valley rim into Lost Arrow notch, the cleft between tower and massif. But the extreme exposure was 'terrifying even for those who had climbed the Cathedral Spires. It was unanimously agreed that we would never attempt it.' Still curious, two years later Leonard returned with David Brower and together they investigated the deep and dark chimneys. These lead in a direct line to the notch which Leonard had already reached on his descent from above. But after climbing no more than 120m, they had to retreat.

They didn't return probably because Leonard thought the route was only climbable with an excessive use of pitons. Leonard disliked pitons and so the deep chimneys of Lost Arrow Spire had to wait for a new period: the era of John Salathé.

Salathé, born near Basle in 1899, left Switzerland after an apprenticeship as a blacksmith at the age of twenty-three without ever having come into contact with the mountains. His route led him across the Atlantic and to Montreal from where he soon moved to the US. In 1932 he ended his travels when he established a blacksmith's workshop in San Mateo, a small town just to the south of San Francisco. But the profession ruined his health and after thirteen years he changed his life radically. According to Steve Roper, Salathé said that a voice had spoken to him: 'John, look at those healthy animals. They eat grass, not meat. You eat meat and you are always feeling sick.'[4] Salathé thus became a vegetarian and thereafter kept in close contact with his 'angel'. He also took up mountaineering. Nobody knows what changed his life for the better, maybe the climbing, maybe the vegetarian food or the help of the angels. Most important was that he regained his physical health after only a few months.

At forty-six years of age with a somewhat eccentric manner he seemed an unlikely candidate for leading an advance in climbing. But there was a driven climber inside, yearning for adventure. He had quickly learned the basics of climbing. Though never regarded as a great free climber, he nevertheless repeated most of the important routes in a short time. In total contrast to Dick Leonard, John Salathé had no qualms about using pitons to make progress and in this he caught the spirit of the age. As a blacksmith Salathé knew that the European soft steel pitons obtainable on the market were unsuitable for repeated use in hard granite. He therefore forged his own pitons from the harder steel used for auto-axles, and these were to give him a great advantage in the climbs he was soon to attempt. In hindsight this can now be seen as a fortuitous event – a blacksmith arriving in Yosemite just at the moment that big wall climbs were being considered. The scale and blankness of the Valley's granite walls meant that climbers would need to use and remove pitons repeatedly. In Europe the leading rock climbers had mainly been operating on limestone which required pitons to be used occasionally, usually on overhangs or for belay, abseil or pendulum anchors, and they were often left in place. Salathé's innovations would eventually revolutionise piton designs around the world.

By 1946, Salathé was ready to attempt Lost Arrow Spire. He arranged to team up with two other climbers but they did not arrive. Others in this situation may have opted to wait for another opportunity. Not Salathé. He abseiled solo from the plateau down the vertical granite wall to the Lost Arrow notch. A thin ledge stretches from the notch out to the left and across above a merciless exposure of granite falling in one big drop to the Valley floor. Salathé having not yet seen enough, roped up and traversed out onto the ledge with the aid of a primitive self-belay. Twenty-five metres above him, he could see another ledge. Could he get up there? He had to try. A narrow crack stretched up above. It was time to use his new pitons. Without these, he would have been unable to make progress. He made it to just short of the ledge and was then forced to place his first bolt. The process of self-belaying on a solo climb, using artificial climbing techniques and placing bolts all took time. It was already late afternoon as he reached the upper ledge – now known as the Salathé Ledge. He knew that he would not make it that day so he abseiled back to the notch and using prusik knots made his way back to the rim. One week after his solo attempt, he went back, this time with John Thune. Just twelve metres

from the summit, darkness forced them to turn back. The only hope would have been time-consuming bolting but it was too late in the day. They decided to end this attempt but resolved to return as soon as possible.

Unfortunately for Salathé four prolific Valley climbers – Anton Nelson, Fritz Lippmann, Jack Arnold and Robin Hansen – got wind of events and guessed that Salathé would soon gain the top of Lost Arrow Spire. What followed was astounding but had little to do with genuine climbing. The four men spent a whole day launching a rope over the top of the Lost Arrow Spire, which reached all the way down the other side to the Salathé Ledge. The next day, Nelson and Arnold abseiled into the notch and attempted the twenty-five-metre pitch to the Salathé Ledge. Lacking the hard pitons, they failed where Salathé had succeeded single-handedly. After a night spent in the notch, a further rope was slung to help them over the missing ten metres to the Salathé Ledge. They reached the rope hanging over the summit and with that, the route to the top was clear. Jack Arnold made it first to the tip of Lost Arrow Spire on 2 September using prusik loops.

The way in which the last unclimbed pinnacle in Yosemite was ascended was certainly not done in the spirit of the age. Salathé himself regarded it merely as cheap rope trick and felt the Lost Arrow still awaited a proper ascent. For a while, however, he turned his attention elsewhere to the second "big challenge" of those times: The South-West Face of Half Dome. This face had already defeated most of the big names in climbing in the 1930s – Eichorn, Robinson, Leonard, Brower – none of them getting further than fifty metres up the wall.

In October 1946, Salathé persuaded the very man who grabbed Lost Arrow Spire from under his nose,

Lost Arrow Spire

Below: John Salathé and Yvon Chouinard

Anton Nelson, to join him on his Half Dome attempt. The two followed a system of cracks, which stretched the full length of the face. These were very thin but once again Salathé's pitons proved to be the key to success. The short days of October meant Salathé and Nelson were forced to make a standing bivouac (a first in Yosemite) on the face just short of where the easier summit slopes began. In the early hours of the following morning, after a night spent upright, the two men reached the summit of Half Dome. Although not a particularly steep route and only 300m long, this was considered one of the toughest climbs in America at the time, due solely to its highly technical pitches (A3/5.7 now 5.10)

It was clear to them both that they made a good team. The plan for next year had to be the "true" conquest of Lost Arrow Spire from the bottom and without omitting the dreaded Lost Arrow Chimneys. They knew that they would be spending several days on the wall before they might eventually succeed. This was going to be a "big wall". They made several attempts during the summer of 1947 until they finally won through in September. Salathé took eight hours to complete the fifty-metre crux pitch of Lost Arrow Chimney. This time it was not just his special pitons but his incredible determination which ensured their success. On the morning of the fifth day, only ten metres left remained. Several hours and bolts later, Salathé and Nelson finally stood astride the tiny summit of Lost Arrow Spire.

For such a "big wall", as it is termed, Salathé and Nelson had very little gear with them. Along with Salathé's new invention, the "skyhook", they only had 18 pitons, 12 karabiners, 18 bolts, a climbing rope, a haul rope, 4 kilos of food and 6 litres of water. And that was for two people for five days! In every respect, this had to be the most magnificent climb of its day. America's first big wall route was longer, tougher, more complex and scarier than any other to date (A3/5.8 now 5.10). It also represented the peak of Salathé's climbing career. But there was still more to come. Having already climbed two of the three "last great problems" in Yosemite, the Sentinel had to be next.

Many attempts had been made on the 500m North Face of the Sentinel during the late 1940s. It is a sheer, smooth, vertical granite wall. Allen Steck, together with Jim Wilson had already managed the first 150m including the first crux point, a squeeze chimney just above the Wilson Overhang. Steck recalled Salathé's prowess on Lost Arrow Spire and Half Dome and promptly gave him a call to suggest a partnership. At fifty-one years of age, Salathé was still easily enlisted.

In true Salathé style, the two set off on 30 June 1950 with just 18 pitons, 15 karabiners, 12 bolts, 10 litres of water and minimal provisions. Two days later they were already breaking new ground, just above the Flying Buttress. Despite an incredible heat wave, they climbed on as Steck related:

'… it was just too damned hot. Each afternoon at two the sun came from behind the wall and turned the face into a veritable furnace. Temperatures up to 105 degrees were recorded down in the Valley and there wasn't a breath of wind. We could watch the swimmers down in the Valley, languishing in the cold waters of the Merced.'[1]

On the morning of the fourth day, they had reached the start of the chimney system. Steck disappeared thirty metres into and up a narrow tunnel going deep into the cliff and eventually emerged on a thin ledge just below the Narrows.

'… again the same old story – where to go? I can only say that there was little there with which to work. John finally made a bold attempt, using pitons upon which only he would ever rely. Hanging almost horizontal, he was barely able to reach around to the outside of the chimney. The piton crack he found made the lead. The Narrows were behind us!'[1]

The heat began to take its toll. They topped out by noon on the fifth day, but for Steck the tortuous journey was far from over.

'The awful thirst. The overpowering heat cannot be described in simple words. Once on top we could see the thin foam line of the stream down in the gorge. We were on top, sure, but the ordeal wasn't over. We had yet to get down to the water that was staring us in the face … my judgement was numbed by the thought of water. I tripped over bushes, fell over unseen ledges, and finally collapsed fully clothed into a pool at the foot of a small waterfall. This was the climax of the climb, a supreme climax! All I can say, in retrospect, is that it was well worth the effort. The reason, the incentive, the motive for all this? It is an intangible, provocative concept that I shall leave to the reader to explain. Some think they know why; others despair of ever knowing. I'm not too sure myself.'[1]

The 'Narrows' of the Steck/Salathé (5.9) on Sentinel Rock

Below: Sentinel Rock

The first ascent of the Sentinel (A3/5.9 now 5.10a) was to be Salathé's last big adventure. Growing more eccentric, he gradually distanced himself from what had been an intense period in his life. Despite the relatively short time he had spent climbing, his five-year span left him with quite a string of successes to his name. His first ascents not only captured all the then feasible big walls of Yosemite but were done in true pioneering spirit. Every wall was tackled alpine style with the use of a minimal amount of gear. His constant search for better tools also led the way for a universal reduction in the use of bolts. The manner in which Salathé tackled the greatest problems made him a legend.

ALLEN STECK ON THE STECK/SALATHÉ

In July 2001, at the age of seventy-five, Allen Steck stood at the foot of Sentinel with Andy Selters. Fifty-one years after the first ascent with Salathé, Steck wanted to climb it again. Even though the chimneys were going to be extremely tiring he could not be dissuaded. Two-thirds of the climb went by without a problem. By late afternoon they were at the start of the Narrows. Selters led up past this crux point but their haul sack got stuck in the narrowest part of the chimney. Steck tried to squeeze himself into the chimney in order to free the sack but simply couldn't manage it. Steck described his predicament to me in a letter:

> 'I had to set up a bivouac there and then, right in the middle of the Narrows! No food, no water and no jacket – everything was in the haul sack, which now hung just above my head. It started off relatively warm but by midnight I was chilled to the bone. I could not sleep and spent the whole night trying to figure out how to get out of this mess. By helicopter? Via mountain rescue? Or else I'd simply have to die here. By morning, I felt more positive. With the help of an ample pull on the rope from above, I finally made it through the chimney.'

Half Dome in the evening light

5 THE GOLDEN AGE

John Salathé's first ascents had opened climbers' eyes. The aura of impossibility surrounding the high walls of Cathedral Rocks, Half Dome and El Capitan was now changing into the realm of the possible.

Whereas in Europe the Golden Age of alpine climbing had reached its peak back in 1865 with the first ascent of the Matterhorn, nearly a hundred years later Yosemite's Golden Age was starting to unfold. Unlike Europe however, Yosemite was not about the first ascents of peaks. The summit (or tip) of the last important unclimbed peak, Lost Arrow Spire, had been 'reached' ten years earlier. Yosemite's attraction and challenge lay in its countless difficult, huge granite walls. One by one, all of these big walls were mastered, in a saga that was to make Yosemite a household name in the climbing world.

In the same manner as the Golden Age of alpine climbing, Yosemite's Golden Age also attracted its own group of protagonists. These included pioneers whose visionary attitudes and skills pushed back the boundaries of the achievable.

The most respected figure in the Golden Age was Royal Robbins. He was the acknowledged leader of the Valley climbing scene over a span of nearly twenty years and encouraged adventure with his ethical and sporting view on how to climb big walls.

Robbins left home at a young age, due to difficult family circumstances. At sixteen he had already quit school and was well on his way to getting to where he wanted to be – the outdoors! He worked in ski resorts during the winter and spent his summers climbing. He showed great talent, earning the respect of all with his free ascent of the Open Book (5.9) in 1952 at the age of seventeen. A well-known technical route on the granite of Tahquitz Rock, east of Los Angeles, it was considered to be the hardest free climb of its day.

One year later he paid his first visit to Yosemite Valley with a group of Tahquitz climbers. His aim was the second ascent of the Steck/Salathé on the Sentinel. They duly made the repeat. Together with Jerry Gallwas and Don Wilson, Robbins managed to shorten the time to just two days. They free climbed almost all the way and found a variation to the original line by the claustrophobic chimney, the Narrows, which today forms part of the normal route.

Just two years later, Robbins left his own personal mark on Yosemite. Discussions around the fire in Camp 4 were increasingly centred on the 1954 failed first attempt on the North-West Face of Half Dome. Climbers had only managed sixty metres of the climb. Robbins saw this as his chance and sought out a strong partner to join him – Warren Harding. Second only to Robbins, Harding was to become another of the legendary figures of the era. In appearance, he was seductively demonic in contrast with the almost saintly dignity of Robbins.

Harding's post-climbing antics made as much a name for him as Robbins' purist attitudes worked for him. He was the real "free spirit" on the scene. Fast cars, red wine, wild parties and lots of women. A lateral thinker, Harding hated any kind of rules and actively shunned anything which would hamper his freedom. Whilst others would immerse themselves in great debates on ethics, Harding would prefer to immerse himself in a good party. His climbing methods were also offensive to some of the "Valley Christians" as he called them. He could not have cared less what other climbers thought of the siege tactics he used to get up his climbs.

In 1955, however, when Harding and Robbins were still Yosemite novices, the differences between the two were not yet apparent. So, along with Gallwas and Wilson, they set off on the North-West Face of Half Dome. Just as their predecessors had experienced, progress was slow and they struggled to advance. Three days later and only 150m above the start they gave up well below the main difficulties.

Two years later, Robbins and Gallwas had far from forgotten the wall and its difficulties. They began thorough preparations for a further attempt in June 1957. They forged their own Lost Arrows as well as early Knife Blades. On 24 June, Mike Sherrick joined them for the next attempt. With the knowledge gained on their previous attempt, they reached the 1955 highpoint on the first day. Their progress was swift and by the second day they had already climbed 300m and now stood facing a compact and featureless wall. Above them to their right lay a set of chimneys that presented the obvious route to follow. After placing seven bolts, Robbins was in a position to see that below him to the right was a small ledge leading to the chimneys. Sherrick lowered Robbins ten metres from the highest bolt. On this ridiculously exposed wall, Robbins then began to run back and forth making several attempts to get a handhold until he finally reached the ledge. With this, the most extreme pendulum traverse to date in Yosemite, Robbins found the key to the next section of the wall. On the fourth day, Gallwas mastered the next hard section: the celebrated cracks known today as the Zig-Zags, a feature created by the large-scale exfoliation of Half Dome's granite mass. Then, on the fifth day, just as progress again grew more questionable, a solution appeared as if on cue. At the end of the Zig-Zags, a horizontal ledge, the Thank God Ledge appeared on the left, about fifteen metres long getting narrower as it went. This

weakness allowed progress across the steep summit overhang known as the Visor, first by precarious walking, then on one's knees, and finally by hand-traversing – all on the most exposed part of the wall.

After this marvellous climax to a fine climb the three men reached the summit just before dark, to complete the first ascent of the great face of Half Dome (A3/5.8 now A1/5.8), at that time the longest and hardest rock climb in North America. Warren Harding was waiting for them at the top to offer his warmest congratulations on their great success.

Harding, with Mark Powell and Bill "Dolt" Feuerer, had also come to Yosemite with the North-West Face of Half Dome in mind but they arrived too late. Ambitious dreamer that Harding was, he was left deeply wounded by the loss of this first ascent. Despite this, he did not bear a grudge – at least not in public – showing noble character. Back in the Valley, Harding drove straight to El Cap Meadows, and gazed up at the monolith-like granite wall in front of him. There were plenty of challenging goals to undertake, but apart from El Capitan nothing compared with the North-West Face of Half Dome. To appease his soul, he had no option but to take on the last great problem – The Nose of El Capitan, the greatest of Yosemite's big walls.

Warren Harding

6 EL CAPITAN[7]

I suppose this article could be titled "The Conquest of El Capitan". However, as I hammered in the last bolt and staggered over the rim, it was not at all clear to me who was conqueror and who was conquered: I do recall that El Cap seemed to be in much better condition than I was.

The above mentioned last bolt marked the conclusion of a venture that began in July 1957. Mark Powell, Bill "Dolt" Feuerer and I met in Yosemite Valley intending an attempt on the North Face of Half Dome. We discovered that an excellent team of climbers from southern California was already at work on it and had the situation well in hand. In our disappointment, we became a bit rash and decided to "have a go" at El Cap.

I'm sure no climber ever considered El Cap impossible – the term "impossible climb" having long since become obsolete. The fact that, previously, there had been no serious attempts to scale the sheer 2900-foot face was simply due to the common belief among rock climbers that techniques were not sufficiently advanced to cope with such a problem.

After we decided to attempt the climb, we spent an entire day studying the face in search of a continuous route to the summit. It was obvious that existing methods of conducting a sustained rock climb would be inadequate. Because of the extreme difficulty of the climbing we anticipated slow progress – perhaps no more than 100 to 200 feet a day. We would spend many days on the rock, so reasonably comfortable campsites were a necessity.

Unfortunately there appeared to be very few ledges. We agreed unanimously that the only feasible plan of attack would be to establish a succession of camps

7 Abridged from the article in the 1959 *American Alpine Journal*.

up the face, linking them with fixed ropes. Supplies would be hauled up from the ground as needed. This would require a support party to assemble and tie loads to our hauling lines. Our technique was to be similar to that used in ascending high mountains, with prusiking and rappelling gear replacing ice axe and crampons as aids for travelling, and winch and hauling lines instead of Sherpas.

On 4 July 1957, we began hammering our way up the smooth, glacier-polished wall. There was no thought of reaching the summit on this attempt – our tentative goal was El Cap Towers, the prominent pinnacle on the east side of the buttress about half way up the face.

On the third day we reached Sickle Ledge, 550 feet up, and established Camp I. The next four days were spent pushing the route upward toward the Towers. The climbing was almost entirely sixth class, direct aid and about as difficult as can be imagined. Finally, 150 feet short of the lower tower, we were forced to give up. Our special "stoveleg" pitons which had brought us up 300 feet of the two- to three-inch-wide Stoveleg Crack were so battered that they would no longer hold.

Leaving fixed ropes behind to secure what we had gained, we descended. Reaching the ground, our spirits were somewhat dampened by an unexpected problem. It seemed that our climbing presented quite a spectacle and had attracted a crowd of tourists which created a traffic jam at the road junction near the base. The Park Rangers were understandably distressed and we had to agree to stay off the rock during the tourist season, between Memorial Day and Labor Day. This meant we would be climbing with shorter days and less certain weather. Difficulties of the El Capitan ascent were not confined to the rock!

Early hauling methods on El Capitan: (far left) the pram-wheeled Dolt Cart with load; (near left) the cart's elevating gantry

According to our agreement, nothing was done until after Labor Day. Beginning with a four-day tour at Thanksgiving, there was a series of attritional attacks extending through October 1958, which whittled away the remaining 2000 feet to a point which a final push might stand a chance of success.

Limited space prevents adequate description of the troubles and frustrations that plagued us in the next several months. About everything that could go wrong did. The first blow, and probably the worst, was Powell's unfortunate accident. In September 1957, he took a bad fall (while on an easy climb) and fractured and dislocated his ankle, putting himself out of action for a long time, if not permanently. Then, weather in the spring and early fall of 1958 was abominable. New equipment such as the winch, laboriously carted 1200 feet up to Dolt Tower, was not nearly as effective as it might have been.

Along with the new equipment, new faces appeared on the rock. This too, posed a problem. Powell and Feuerer felt no new members should be admitted to the group. I didn't think the three of us constituted a strong enough party to go ahead on El Cap, since Powell, who had climbed brilliantly on the first attempt, was no longer capable of doing much leading. The dissension arising from this situation ultimately resulted in Powell and Feuerer dropping out, except for the continued use of Feuerer's pitons and other special equipment. So I continued with whatever "qualified" climbers I could "con" into this rather unpromising venture.

By mid-October 1958, Camp IV at 1800 feet level and a high point at 200 feet, just below the Great Roof, had been established. The Chief Ranger had given us a deadline – to complete the climb by Thanksgiving. I have never understood how this was

to have been enforced. But it didn't matter; we were all determined to reach the summit before winter.

After a long, hard look at the remaining 900 feet of the upper face, Wayne Merry, George Whitmore, Rich Calderwood and I agreed that an all-out effort was in order. On 1 November 1958 we started up the fixed ropes for what we hoped would be the last time. The weather had cleared and the invigoratingly cool breezes were a pleasant contrast to the violent thunderstorms and oppressive heat of the nine-day effort in September. Due to a late start, we reached Camp IV a little after dark and were soon in our sleeping bags discussing plans for the next day.

Next morning we ascended the fixed line to the previous high point and went to work on the long-dreaded Roof Pitch. While strenuous and just a bit scary – nailing around the right side of the 180-degree overhang with 2000 feet of space directly below – it proved to be not nearly as difficult as we had thought it would be. The following seven days blurred into a monotonous grind – if living and working 2500 feet above ground on a vertical granite face can be considered monotonous! On Sunday evening, the ninth day, a storm broke, providing a welcome day of rest from the hammering and hauling.

While sitting out the storm at Camp VI, Wayne and I took stock of the situation. Except for Rich Calderwood, who had gone down with an attack of nerves, we were all in good condition. Whitmore was somewhere down below, most likely Camp IV, and would be coming up with another load of food. We had been working out of Camp VI for the past three days and, while we were not certain, we felt that our high point was surely no more than a couple of hundred feet below the rim. A determined push might

put us over the top in one more day. We liked the thought, anyway. We were getting just a little tired of the whole thing.

By Tuesday morning the storm had blown itself out. After shouting our plans down to George, Wayne and I left Camp VI with extra food and batteries for our headlamps. Mid-morning found us at our high point and pushing on. As we began nailing up the next pitch, we heard a most welcome sound – a yodel from the top! John Whitmer, Ellen Searby and Rick Anderson had hiked in to meet us. Spurred on by the encouraging knowledge that we actually were near the rim, we hammered up the next two pitches with enthusiasm if not speed. It was nearly four o'clock when we reached the tiny ledge that would serve as a belay-spot for the last pitch.

We could now see John and Ellen peering down at us. Also visible was the route between us and the top – a most impressive-looking pitch! The crack ended under an overhanging wall that was ninety-feet high and completely devoid of cracks – 15 pitons, 28 bolts and 14 hours were required to surmount that final pitch. But at six the next morning I pulled over the top and stared feebly at Ellen as she struggled with her camera's faulty flash-attachment.

7 Camp 4 — The New Home

Just as the first ascent of the North-West Face of Half Dome affected the climbing world, so too The Nose (A3/5.8 now A2/5.8 or mainly free at 5.11) left people with a feeling that anything was now possible.

The climb was not just of interest in the climbing world either. It turned into quite a media spectacle. "Yosemite Climbers Make It", "El Capitan Conquered" being typical headlines from California's leading newspapers, whose reports for the very first time provided a popular insight into this crazy sport of the great outdoors. Front pages were filled with photographs of Harding, tired and drawn, wearily pulling himself up onto the summit plateau of El Capitan. *The San Francisco Chronicle* published no less than eight days of reportage on the successful ascent of The Nose.

Most climbers were contemptuous of the publicity which Harding attracted. For them, climbing was a "pure" sport with the natural setting and the climbers themselves sufficing. Recognition should only be sought in their own circles.

Harding however, was not shy of publicity. Shortly after his return to the Valley, he was on the phone. *Life* magazine and other magazines and newspapers paid thousands of dollars for photos of The Nose. The climbing press abstained. No mention of the ascent of The Nose was made in either the *Sierra Club Bulletin* or *Summit*, the only regularly published magazines on the sport. Only in 1959 did an article entitled "El Capitan" appear in the *American Alpine Journal.*

Despite or perhaps as a direct reaction to all the fuss over The Nose, most climbers remained rather detached from the big wall developments and chose instead to stick to their own climbing.

The start of the Golden Age also coincided with a change in the climbers' lifestyle. Whereas they had previously only been visitors to the park, they now occupied Camp 4 throughout the whole summer and fall. In addition to weekend climbers, there was now a core group of climbers for whom Yosemite was home. These "residents" knew that by choosing this way of life, they didn't even have to hold down a full-time job in order to live well. And life in the Valley certainly proved to be cheap. Without a car, without any form of insurance and living "rent-free" in Camp 4, life was good. Making their own food over campfires, one dollar a day was enough to survive on. The Yosemite residents got casual work in the winter, saving up a few hundred dollars and with that, they managed to survive a further eight months or so pursuing the important thing in life: Climbing!

With climbing going on every day for a whole season, climbing know-how took a huge upturn. It comes as no surprise then, that the example set by the first "residents" and an ever-expanding community in Camp 4 very quickly led to important results. The first resident of the time was Mark Powell. As an overweight beginner in 1956, his first climbing excursion turned into quite a fiasco. His movements were laboured, his climbing positively awful and he spent most of his time relying heavily on the rope rather than the holds. After that, Powell decided to take drastic action, putting himself on a strict diet and gearing his whole life towards climbing. That winter he saved up some money and then spent a few months in the summer of 1957 in Yosemite. It wasn't long before people looked on with sheer awe. Powell became one of the driving forces in climbing! Almost sensing that his glory days were numbered, he whirled his way through the Yosemite walls like a restless creature. In just fifteen months, usually in

Face of Fairview Dome (A1/5.8 now 5.9), the largest wall in Tuolumne. Pratt's climbing style was very natural. Although very powerfully athletic, he knew how to move economically on a wall, without showing any visible signs of physical strain. Pratt's eye for interesting and rewarding routes also had an impact on climbing.

The Golden Age was not only the time of spectacular big wall climbing but also a period of growth in short but tough free climbs on the smaller walls in Yosemite. These only became popular much later. Reed and Pratt, for example, added climbs on Cookie Cliff, Elephant Rock and Reed's Pinnacle. The end was not the goal on these routes. A distant summit was not important, it was more the difficulty of the climb that was its attraction, though others used these routes as training grounds for big walls. Whatever the driving force, the trend became established and Reed, Pratt and their now expanding circle of followers relentlessly made one first ascent after another of climbs that were mainly based on cracks. As their skills grew they were soon free climbing routes previously viewed with great trepidation.

Despite this activity on shorter free climbs, the focus remained on the mixed free and aid climbs on the big walls. Warren Harding made the most important first ascent in 1959 using his expedition style, the 300m East Face of the Washington Column (A3/5.9 now A1/5.9 or free at 5.11c). Harding had started the route in the summer of 1958 during one of the enforced breaks in his El Capitan ascent, and he returned after his fixed ropes had been left untouched for a whole year. Just above the end of the fixed rope was a four-metre overhanging roof, cross-sectioned by a funnel-like chimney. True to his style, Harding used technical moves to work his way into the chimney until a piton

partnership with Wally Reed, he had mastered no fewer than fifteen first ascents. Then, sadly, he had a bad fall on Arrowhead Spire, leaving him with complicated fractures and with that, his exploratory climbing career was effectively over.

But the Golden Age was now in full swing. And when one climber's career ends due to injury, marriage or change of occupation, others soon embark on that same road of packing up their job, university and girlfriend to move into the Valley.

In this vein, the nineteen-year-old Chuck Pratt quit his studies in 1958 and with several friends moved into the Valley. It wasn't long before he ranked next to Robbins as one of the most talented and versatile climbers of the period. Wally Reed, in the meantime, had been the first to recognise the potential in the granite domes of the Tuolumne Meadows. In Pratt, Reed found the enthusiastic partner he had been looking for to tackle the first ascent of the North

failed, together with several previous placements and he was spat out into the void. He was only lightly injured but very shaken and so they decided to retreat.

In July Harding still yearned to complete the route. In his search for partners, he stumbled across Pratt and Steve Roper (another of the most talented new climbing residents) in Camp 4. They were the only ones who had stayed behind in the Valley during the unbearable heat. They had no money to go elsewhere and so just sat and waited for something to happen. Harding turned up with a couple of bottles of wine and in his own charming and persuasive way, convinced the two to join him on his mission.

They say, the easiest way to a man's heart is through his stomach. To this end, Harding bought the two hungry men with gifts of food. On 21 July, hauling vast amounts of kit and water, they made their way up to the Harding Slot. By the afternoon the dreaded passage lay behind them. To this day, climbers still rarely escape unscathed from that frighteningly narrow squeeze chimney. In fact, the whole of the East Face had its moments and was so problematic that it took nine days to get up its 300 metres! Early on, they realised that Roper, serving as their only sherpa was just not enough and so others were summoned to help. On 29 July 1959, Harding, Pratt and sherpa/photographer Glen Denny completed the face with the fixed rope spanned from bottom to top.

True to Harding's style, his first ascent was splashed over the front page of the *Oakland Tribune* the very next day. Harding had sent Roper down to the Valley with a roll of film the day before they topped out.

CAMP 4 — A NATIONAL HISTORIC PLACE

Disastrous floods in January 1997 destroyed a great number of the tourist facilities in Yosemite National Park. According to the National Park Service, plans had been made to re-erect these in the flood-proof woods of Camp 4. Tom Frost got wind of these plans during a big wall climbing trip to the Valley with his son Ryan. He immediately enlisted the services of lawyer/climber Dick Duane to stop the destruction of Camp 4.

A meeting was held between American Alpine Club members and National Park Service officials and Frost fought the climbers' case:

> 'We love you all as people. But your plans are wrong. In rearranging the buildings in the Valley, you are in effect rearranging the deck chairs on the *Titanic*. The NPS 'ship' is sailing on the wrong ocean, and we want to help you find your way back.'

Signed petitions from climbers all over the world were gathered as well as statements from organisations such as the UIAA and a strategy was formed to protect Camp 4. Dick Duane, in what had now developed into a lengthy episode, managed to get them to concede that the site was of "unusual significance in relation to modern-day climbing".

The judge in charge of the proceedings paid a visit to Camp 4 to see just what all the fuss was about. He agreed the site was unique due to its special history and declared Camp 4 a "National Historic Place".

The National Park Service then merged the plans of the American Alpine Club with their own – Camp 4 was saved!

To celebrate their victory, the whole of the climbing world, including most of the legendary figures, gathered at Camp 4 in September 1999. It was a momentous occasion in the history of climbing. During the celebrations, the National Park Service also announced that "Sunnyside", the name given to the site in 1971, would once again be known as "Camp 4".

One of the residents: Chongo Chuck

*Scotty's camp on top of El Capitan – (left to right)
Scotty Burk, Thomas and Alexander Huber and
Leo Houlding*

Bear-proof trunk

*Left: The American way of life – getting ready for a big
wall in Camp 4*

Below: The Mountain Room bar

53

El Cid in attack mode

(below) The John Muir tree

THE BEARS' VERY OWN CAMP 4

Rather unfairly, the rangers tend to be viewed as the greatest threat in Camp 4, but it is more often the bears that make climbers' lives difficult. The relatively small population of bears in Yosemite does not generally pose a threat to humans, but when they leave the High Sierra in search of anything edible, night after night Camp 4 is robbed. Anything not locked away in bear-proof lockers is at risk. Unfortunately for the climbers, it doesn't take much more effort on the part of the bears to tear open a car than it does in getting into a tin can.

During the 1960s the climbers had even given names to the greatest perpetrators: Spartacus, Caligula, Lancelot and El Cid. Serial robbers, all of them, they were still clever

enough not to conduct raids on consecutive nights. Sometimes a whole week went by before they would strike again. Steve Roper recounts:

'One evening, TM Herbert had endured enough. He positioned himself atop the Wine Traverse Boulder cradling a huge rock waiting for El Cid who often ambled by this particular boulder at dusk. Sure enough, along came the creature and down crashed the stone onto Cid's skull. A perfect knockout strike! A small "click" resulted. El Cid looked around, shook his massive head twice, and then waddled into camp to see what was cooking.'[4]

Cathedral Rocks

8 BIG WALLS — HARDING VERSUS ROBBINS

The Nose had to wait nearly two years for its second ascent. In 1960 Robbins seized the opportunity. True to his philosophy on climbing, he waited until he felt in a position to do the route without the aid of fixed ropes. In Joe Fitschen, Tom Frost and Chuck Pratt he had selected the strongest climbers around at the time. A team of four would make the task much easier. Two could concentrate purely on the climbing while the other two could haul the 60 litres of water and 40kg of equipment needed for ten days on El Capitan. This promised to be even harder work than the climbing itself. They had 7 climbing ropes, 2 haul ropes, 67 karabiners and 100 pitons. They expected to be much faster than Harding's team but all four were amazed when they reached the Valley rim after just seven days.

This second ascent of The Nose confirmed the wisdom of Robbins's style and ethics and proved to be a seminal event in big wall climbing. Viewed from the outside, it was simply four talented climbers who had succeeded in getting up the world's biggest and steepest rock-climb in a relatively short time and without too much strain. Harding and his friends had done the route-finding and the various technical sections so the second ascent was bound to be faster. Nevertheless informed climbers knew that after Harding's first ascent, another boundary had been crossed and El Capitan should no longer be an expedition-style target. Robbins's team had proved that it was possible to climb El Capitan stylishly, without excessive fixed roping.

The stage was now set for Robbins to leave his own mark on El Capitan. He located the next weak spot in the middle of the awesome South-West Face, which even before its first ascent had become known as Salathé Wall. This started not far to the left of The Nose and followed a line that seemed to end in an impenetrable barrier of walls. At the start of September 1961, Robbins, Frost and Pratt finally 'came to the giddy conclusion that a magnificent route lay here'.

The expedition style of using long extensions of fixed rope was out of the question for Robbins, so fixed ropes were only used on the lower third of the wall so that they could then climb from there straight to the top. This approach, though not perfect, earned the three so much respect that their methods were soon adopted as the accepted style for multi-day projects. Robbins explained that 'this plan seemed the best compromise between what was possible and our dour desire to keep the enterprise as adventurous as we could.'[4]

So with the necessary extra ropes (for fixing) in their packs, they set off on the lower section of the wall. At 150m above the start, just before the obvious features of Half Dollar and Mammoth Terraces, they had to place thirteen bolts in blank sections of slabs. These were to be the only bolts used on the whole route. On the fourth day they reached Heart Ledges. They fixed their ropes down from these wide ledges at the lower end of the massive, heart-shaped formation in the middle of the wall, and went back down to the Valley floor.

Three days later, using their fixed ropes, the trio were back at the Heart Ledges. With just three ropes left they set off into the unknown. In the same uncompromising style as Salathé, they severed their links to the world below and climbed pitch after pitch upwards. In this way, had they been struck by bad weather or made slow progress, it would have meant aborting their attempt and having to make a difficult retreat. But they all agreed this style of ascent was right — total siege-style on such a wall

Leaning Tower

would remove the uncertainty and make the climbing boring.

It took them six days to climb the remaining 700m of impressively steep granite to the summit of El Capitan. The first obstacle they encountered was the dreaded Hollow Flake, still feared today. Robbins overcame this by a pendulum traverse into the flake and he then climbed its twenty-metre offwidth crack without any chance to place protection. One look down, at the end of the pitch leaves any climber with the realisation that one wrong move at this stage would most certainly mean hospitalisation.

Their greatest obstacle still awaited them just below the summit – a four-metre overhanging roof and the following eighty metres of constantly overhanging headwall. They followed up the perfect splitter crack, the only feature in this overhanging wave of granite. Hanging above the seemingly bottomless void they worked their way up as Robbins described:

> 'There was one point when I was hanging from two pitons on the wall. Chuck had just cleaned the pitch and was above me. They fixed the lines for me, and I got my prusik knots fixed. I was so frightened that I tied a big knot in the end of the rope as well. Finally, I let myself out on the end of the rope for about eight feet; I thought that that would be about right, so I let the rope slip through the piton, but it had been holding me in so much that I swung twenty feet out from the wall – 2500 feet above the ground.'[5]

By the afternoon of 24 September, they reached the summit of what later became lauded as 'the best climb on the planet'. For the first ascent of Salathé Wall (A4/5.9 now A2/5.9) Robbins, Frost and Pratt spent nine-and-a-half days on the wall and used only the thirteen bolts to cross the lower slabs.

> 'Could Harding have done this? Of course not' wrote Steve Roper. 'Would Valley climbing have suffered if Harding had spent a couple of years fixing the route and placing scores of bolts? Absolutely. The time was ripe for evolution. Harding pioneered the big-wall concept. Robbins refined it.'[4]

Steve Roper's comments express the views of many of the Valley's climbers, past and present … the Salathé Wall ascent pointed the way to an heroic new future for climbing.

Harding's answer to Robbins's newest triumph was soon to follow. His next creation, the West Face of the Leaning Tower (A4/5.5 now A2/5.5), was a demonstration of all that Robbins decried – 110 bolts and 350m of fixed rope were placed during the numerous attempts.

The Leaning Tower is located on the southern slopes of the Valley, right next to the spectacular Bridalveil Fall. The West Face is continuously overhanging, at an angle of up to twenty degrees over the vertical on the lower section. Furthermore the granite was exceptionally featureless and it was obvious this would require many bolts. So, of all the walls, why did Harding choose this particular one? His answer was simply that 'It was a face I'd long wanted to do.' There was nothing for it, he collected as many climbing partners and as much gear as possible and with his usual tenacity, bolted his way to the top. This, of course, enraged the other climbers who by now had seen what was possible after the Salathé success.*

* All of the Leaning Tower, West Face (except the first pitch) was freed in May 2001 by Leo Houlding and Jason Pickles at 5.13b (E7, 6c).

Even greater controversy followed. Two climbers from the Northwest, Ed Cooper from Seattle and Jim Baldwin from Canada, came to Yosemite in 1962 and, after a series of attempts, climbed the big face to the left of Salathé Wall – Dihedral Wall (A3/5.9 now A2/5.8). They did it in thirty-eight days, spread over that year. The fact that one of the locals, Glen Denny, was enlisted into their party still did not stop this ascent also being viewed as a backward step.

Robbins's view on the matter is an accurate portrayal of the sentiment surrounding it at the time:

> 'We were annoyed that an outsider would come in, after we thought we had put siege climbing to sleep, and force this route up El Cap which we felt should have been done in the right style.'[5]

In the Valley, much more value was placed on how you climbed rather than what you climbed. The differences in opinion on what was "correct" conduct drove a rift into the whole climbing community.

> 'Before 1962, relationships among climbers had been remarkably friendly with little friction and enormous respect' Steve Roper related. 'Subtly, this began to change, and part of the reason was an influx of a new group of irreverent climbers. Baldwin and Cooper were one such pair.'[4]

Not every newcomer was criticised. When Layton Kor turned up in Yosemite in the autumn of 1960 he was known as the best climber in Colorado. It was not his reputation that attracted respect but more his attitude to climbing and his ability. Kor was a hugely energetic twenty-two-year-old with impressive speed on rock. As Jim Bridwell described him: 'He was full of positive energy. He was always going! He'd grab anybody to do a route, including me. Kor was a

climbing animal. You'd think he was on speed the way he raced up one route after another!'[5] In 1963 he pulled off his most significant first ascent in Yosemite when, with Steve Roper, he completed the fourth route on El Capitan, the West Buttress (A2/5.9), in just three days.

The next big step was made by Royal Robbins who, climbing alone, became the first to repeat Harding's route on Leaning Tower. It was the first time that one of the big walls in Yosemite had been climbed solo and it earned Robbins even greater respect. By contrast his next mission demonstrated a certain ruthlessness and put him at the centre of a heated debate. In June 1963, with the help of Dick McCracken, he pulled off the first ascent of the centre of the North-West Face of Half Dome (A5/5.9 now A2/5.9). The controversy was because they moved in on a route which had already been started by others. As weekend climbers Ed Cooper and Galen Rowell were unaware of the ethics being fashioned in Camp 4. They set off armed with numerous ropes, climbed a few pitches, placed five bolts in a tough section and ended their attempt leaving a fixed rope for a return. Robbins had been considering that line and so, prompted by what he thought likely to be another backward step, he sought to convince Layton Kor to join him in a takeover of the project. Kor declined feeling that it would be wrong to intrude, but Robbins was able to persuade McCracken and the two set off on the ascent. Without using the fixed rope, they reached the turnaround point of the others fairly quickly and with the placement of just ten more bolts they completed the wall in five days.

There is no doubt that it was done in near perfect first ascent style. Cooper and Rowell would probably have used much fixed rope and many more bolts and a certain amount of time to complete the route which would have gone against the established practices. But Robbins's takeover was also not according to the accepted codes of the day and it was his turn to take the brunt of criticism. Discussions about routes and techniques thus grew more heated. The "good old days" were now long gone. Climbing was no longer just some friends getting together and spending time on rock faces.

Aside from all the competition surrounding the big walls, a new trend began to evolve in 1964, largely propagated by Frank Sacherer. There was nothing new about free climbing (climbs achieved without any resort to aid). Chuck Wilts and Spencer Austin had already done the first major free climb back in 1944, when they climbed the Higher Cathedral Spire (5.9) completely unaided. But at the age of twenty-four, Sacherer ticked off no less than eleven new free climbs in the space of just a few months. Amongst those were shorter routes such as Reed's Direct (5.10a) on Reed's Pinnacle and Moby Dick Ahab (5.10b) and the Sacherer Cracker on the lower wall of El Capitan. But he also captured longer (previously aided) routes such as the Salathé/Nelson (5.10b) on Half Dome, Lost Arrow Chimney (5.10a) and the North-East Buttress of Higher Cathedral Rock (5.10a). Although Robbins's East Chimney (5.10a) on Rixon's Pinnacle and Pratt's Crack of Doom (5.10b) were the first 5.10 routes in the Valley, Sacherer was the only one to climb consistently at that level. The way in which he climbed was, in the true spirit of the times, almost puritanical. Not once in his whole career did he leave any trace of himself behind on a wall. He simply chose his target and climbed it free. *Veni Vidi Vici*. 'Sacherer was the driving force of climbing in the 1960s' said Jim Bridwell. 'He did more to advance free climbing as we know it today than any other single person in America at that time.'[4]

Roper's rather less flattering summary in *Camp 4* noted:

> 'Sacherer was renowned for his sheer drive and feared for his fiery temper, impatience and tantrums. Chouinard was concerned: "he always climbed on the verge of falling over backwards – using no more energy than was necessary to progress and rarely bothering to stop and place protection …" Sacherer repeatedly shocked his climbing partners with this uncompromising style.'

In a vivid recollection, Roper described Sacherer enlisting him for an attempt on Pratt's prestigious and feared Crack of Doom that even Robbins and Kor had avoided. Roper agreed providing that Sacherer led the hard third pitch (5.10), but on the easier but unprotected second pitch Roper baulked and started to descend. 'What the hell are you doing' snarled Sacherer. 'I can't do it' Roper announced, 'I'm coming down'. 'Stay up there, you chickenshit,' Sacherer shrieked. 'I ignored him' said Roper 'fear of death overcoming fear of Sacherer'. Curiously Sacherer did not spring into the lead on this occasion and on the way back to Camp 4 made small talk as if nothing had happened until, as they arrived his face tightened and he turned to Roper and growled 'tell them it was your fault'.[4]

The next big wall to be climbed in the Valley provided the most emphatic confirmation of the big wall ethics held at Camp 4. Surprisingly, it was Harding along with Chuck Pratt and Yvon Chouinard who succeeded in the first ascent of the South Face of Mount Watkins (A4/5.8 now A2/5.9). The man who stood for siege-climbing now found himself in partnership with climbers of real ability for his latest big wall ascent. It was an indicator of Harding's open-mindedness that he chose to climb with partners whose stance on big wall ascents was so different from his. The three men climbed the South Face in one go, without fixed ropes and using very few bolts.

They started their ascent in the mid-July heat and it was soon evident that any difficulties they encountered would not be limited to the climbing itself. Water supplies ran low and progress was slow. By the fourth day, still a full 250m from the summit, their situation grew more critical as Pratt described:

'Warren had nearly fainted several times from the heat, Yvon was speechless with fatigue and I was curled up in a semi-stupor trying to utilize a small patch of shade beneath an overhanging boulder. … For the first time we considered the possibility of retreating, but even that would require another day on the wall. It seemed that those very qualities which had made the climb so appealing might now prove to be our undoing.'[1]

On the fifth and last day, Harding refused to drink any of the water so that the other two, who were leading at the time, would be able to share what was left. On the verge of total exhaustion, they topped out on the evening of 24 July 1964. Despite all the heat and uncertainty, they had completed an extremely demanding route in the best style possible. They were

certain of universal praise. Even Robbins showed his approval. With this outstanding demonstration by Chouinard, Pratt and Harding it seemed that the days of overburdened big wall ascents were over.

One would have thought the Mount Watkins ascent would have been the high point of that year, but Robbins was not about to let the season slip by without setting a milestone of his own.

In the middle of the South-East Face of El Capitan, there is a huge area of black diorite set into the El Capitan golden granite. Robbins noted 'This diorite forms a crude map … hence the name North America Wall'. Although the obvious routes on the South-West Face had been climbed, the South-East Face had remained untouched due to its daunting appearance. In October 1963, Robbins and Glen Denny had climbed the first 200 metres. Cracks they had hoped would serve them well, proved to be pretty useless and these first pitches were thus very technical.

In May 1964, Tom Frost joined forces with them to launch a second attack. In three days, they had climbed 400 metres and were half-way up the wall, when they reached a small ledge known as Big Sur. This was a good base to work from, as the toughest parts were still to come. They abseiled back to the ground without leaving any fixed ropes.

That autumn, Royal Robbins, Tom Frost, Chuck Pratt and Yvon Chouinard went back for what was to prove to be the first ascent of the North America Wall (A5/5.8 now A3/5.8), the greatest big wall ascent of the era.

Royal Robbins

9 NORTH AMERICA WALL

In mid-October the Sierra was still in the grip of an Indian summer. The Merced had lost its earlier vitality and become a trickle amid sand dunes. The evanescent Yosemite Falls, stupendous in June, had disappeared. The oaks and maples were slow to don their fall clothing; and each afternoon haze crept up the western foothills and filled the Valley – a rare occurrence in a normal autumn.

We all felt similarly about the climb – it was not an appealing wall. It did not have the elegance or majesty of the South-West Face. The treacherous dark rock, the difficulty of retreat due to great overhangs and long traverses, the absence of a natural route and finally the apparent necessity for many bolts rendered us not happily enthusiastic about the venture. A large part of our individual selves did not want to attempt this face. But another part was lured on by the challenge of the greatest unclimbed rock wall in North America. Perhaps it would be a greater adventure for its ogreish appearance. But Chouinard forecast our doom. His previous bad luck on El Capitan had convinced him a black cloud hung over him.

We waited for the heat to abate. The South-East Face is peculiarly a heat problem. Its concavity creates an oven sheltered from westerly breezes by the South Buttress. Dwindling time forced us to start. In mid-afternoon of 22 October, with sweat oozing from every pore, we carried supplies to the base of the wall. Tom and Yvon climbed the first pitch and left a rope on it. We then passed the night at the foot of the face. Yvon hardly slept. Next morning with the sun beating upon us, we climbed upward. As Tom led the second pitch, a tiny horn supporting an aid sling broke, causing a fall. His piton held and he passed the difficulty with a skyhook. Chouinard verified my opinion of the third pitch. He called it

the hardest aid pitch of his experience. A short fall was held by a RURP – the Realized Ultimate Reality Piton – a tiny, slightly wedge-shaped piton, normally only used for aid.

Meanwhile, Chuck and I were hauling the party's 200 pounds of food, water and equipment. The heat was withering. Our 60 quarts of water, which gave us each one and a half quarts per day, would not be enough if this persisted. We passed the night on long, narrow Mazatlán Ledge, 500 feet up. Next morning the circles around Yvon's eyes told of another sleepless night. After Chuck led past the cavernous overhang known as the Gulf of California, I pitoned and climbed familiar bolts to Easy Street, a large broken ledge at 700 feet. We doggedly climbed without enthusiasm in the fierce heat, unconsciously saving ourselves for the forbidding problems above.

The heat wave broke on the sixth day. We reluctantly left our cozy ledge and crossed the traverse to our high point. The section above was ugly. Overhanging to the right 400 feet, the Black Dihedral was a rotten mess. Dropped here by the leader were many rocks and huge balls of mud and grass. Luckily, these objects fell harmlessly far out to the side of us below. Chuck and I, doing the hauling that day, sometimes had to let ourselves out as much as fifty feet in order to prusik straight up to the end of a pitch. After dark, we reached the Black Cave, an alcove with no bottom. Here we spent several hours stringing our hammocks and getting settled. By flashlight Tom observed large centipedes on the wall above. At dawn, casually glancing over the sides of our hammocks, we were astonished at the tremendous exposure. The ground was 1600 feet straight below. Suspended over space, we hung one above another, like laundry between tenement flats. Oppressive is the word for the Black Cave. We felt we had climbed

into a *cul de sac*. As we breakfasted on salami, cheese and a mixture of candies and nuts, cirro-stratus began to cover the sky. My wife Elizabeth, through our tiny two-way radio, told us a storm was forecast.

Chuck led the overhang. He pitoned up one side of it and followed a horizontal dike of aplite around the top. Fascinated, we watched the lower part of Chuck's body move sideways thirty feet across our line of vision. Pitonage was very difficult, and Chuck's hauling line hung far out from the wall. When all cracks stopped, he ended the pitch and belayed in slings, thus finishing the most spectacular lead in American climbing.

We all started pushing as fast as safety would allow, for fear of a bivouac on a blank wall in rainstorm. We climbed onward, searching, always searching. Searching for handholds and footholds, for piton cracks and the right piton. And searching ourselves for the necessary human qualities to make this climb possible. Searching for adventure, searching for ourselves, searching for situations which would call forth our total resources. For some it is a search for courage. Perhaps if we can learn to face the dangers of the mountains with equanimity, we can also learn to face with a calm spirit the chilling spectre of the inevitable death.

Rain had begun before we reached the shelter of the Cyclops Eye, well after dark. The Eye is a great hole in the rock, 200 feet high and 30 feet deep. We would be sheltered from the rain as long as the air was still. That evening, we were serenaded through our radio by our good friend Mort Hempel, singing rare and beautiful folk songs. As leaves are wafted by a breeze, so our spirits soared upward on the exquisite melodies of Mort's art.

The rain ceased next morning, but clouds persisted. The forecast was a three-day storm. We had already begun to ration food, so it would be a close contest. Yvon led. He moved with cat-like grace, which belied the difficulty of the free climbing up the loose flakes and shattered black rock. Then Tom nailed horizontally forty feet in a lead of exceptional severity. Late in the day Yvon led to the top of the Eye. This was the sort of pitch one never wants to do again, as it involved placing large angle pitons straight up between loose, overhanging blocks. The return to the bivouac ledge after dark was an exhaustingly slow and hazardous process.

While Chuck and I had been preparing the bivouac at dusk, menacing clouds, like sharks of various sizes racing after their prey, scudded toward us on a strong south wind. That night, the edge of a great storm moved east over California. Throughout central and northern California southerly gales swept the land, and the dry earth soaked up the downpours. As the storm rose to pass the Sierra, the rain turned to snow at 7000 feet. There we sat, in the furious, inky night, lashed by wind and rain, tiny mites tied to a great rock. Yet the rock itself was dwarfed by the majestic whirlpool of air moving out of the Pacific, and this same storm was just a small blotch on the earth's surface. The earth in turn would be a mere dot on the sun, and there are suns many thousands of times larger than that fiery orb giving us life. Mankind is truly insignificant. Man's fate, indeed, is to have to swallow these truths and still live on. If one could only find meaning to make these hard truths of insignificance and omnipresent death acceptable. Where to find this meaning? Again the search … and we climb on.

The storm abated in the morning and through the mist we perceived the Sierra had donned its winter coat of white. We were sodden. Tom especially had had a bad night. The previous day's climbing had been tough and Tom, always a big eater, was suffering from the stringent diet. The new forecast was encouraging. The storm, instead of continuing eastward through California, had taken a north-eastern tack and spared us several days of rain or snow. We climbed on through light shower that day, flabbergasted at the continuing challenges. A climb with such unrelenting difficulties was a new experience to us.

Next morning, nature smiled. The eastern sun, with beams of warmth, cut the crisp clean air, while the white panorama of the High Sierra, the gentle wilderness, stretched from north-east to south-east, a deep blue sky arching above. Half Dome, as ever stood sublime, a new cap of white on its bald head. We felt joyous to be greeted by such a magnificent morning. The beauty, the expectation of certain success and the sun's heat made our blood race. All around us the exquisite splendour of these friendly mountains added to our elation. As John Harlin has said, 'such beauty … turns satisfaction to pure joy.' Six hours later we had overcome the last problems and shook hands on top, happy as pagans.

Tom Frost, Royal Robbins and Yvon Chouinard (just below Robbins) in their hanging bivouac in the Black Cave during the first ascent of North America Wall, El Capitan, in 1964

El Capitan rising above the meadows, Wall of the Early Morning Light takes the sunlit section right of The Nose and the North America Wall traces a line up the grey patch of rock to the right

10 END OF AN ERA

The first ascent of North America Wall was without a doubt the crown jewel of the Golden Age. As a result of that climb Yosemite climbing attracted huge international prestige, a reputation reinforced in Europe by the big wall climbs added to the Petit Dru (1962 and 1965) and the Aiguille du Fou (1963), the first two involving Robbins, the second with Frost in the party. North America Wall was therefore thought to be the hardest rock climb in the world, or as Robbins later remarked: '[The 38th pitch] one of the hardest leads of my experience, was just another pitch on this route.'[7]

For all four of those climbers, it was the peak of their climbing careers and to some extent also a turning point in their lives. For Tom Frost and Chuck Pratt it would be their last ascent of a new big wall route in Yosemite. Even for Yvon Chouinard and Royal Robbins, the first ascents they went on to do, though very fine, never quite matched their pioneering effort on North America Wall.

The climbers who had been the first up the big walls of Yosemite gradually began to withdraw from Valley life. This slow change in generations also marked the beginning of the end of the Golden Age. This did not mean that there was less action in Camp 4. The pioneers were still active but the heyday of first ascents was now over. New milestones would have to be achieved by a new generation of climbers. The big routes of the era were gradually repeated. The number of climbers with the ability to tackle routes on El Capitan grew steadily and the late 1960s thus became a period of consolidation. Most notable in this phase were climbs such as the one-day ascent of the Regular Route on Half Dome by Steve Roper and Jeff Foott in May 1966. In the days before nut and friend protection they made 250 piton placements and cleared them as they went. Another was the solo ascent of the same route, two months later by Eric Beck.

There was only one more big wall route put up El Capitan in the latter half of the 1960s. In 1965, Chouinard joined forces with TM Herbert. Herbert had been around for years but, with the Chouinard/ Herbert (A2/5.8 now A1/5.8) on the Sentinel as his only significant first ascent, he was not considered a key player. He was however, one of the strongest characters in Camp 4. Great hand movements and facial expressions always accompanied the stories he told of his latest climbing adventures. According to Roper he became known as the resident wit of Camp 4 and often had everyone rolling around in mirth. On the subject of Yosemite's toughest cracks: 'Those cracks won't stand a chance' he cried. 'I'll pull 'em apart; I'll smash 'em; 'I'll make 'em scream with pain.'[4]

In June, Chouinard and Herbert began their climb on El Capitan. They completed the thirty-two pitches of the Muir Wall (A4/5.9 now A2/5.9) in just eight days, without any advance preparation or the use of fixed ropes – giving another boost to the now accepted big wall style.

Events surrounding the attempts to climb the South Face of Half Dome were rather more dramatic. In November 1968 Harding and Rowell were high on the wall when a heavy storm swept through the Sierra Nevada. The rock face was soon covered in ice and beating a retreat was out of the question. After two terrible nights in their bivouacs they were suffering from hypothermia and used their radios to call for help. On the afternoon of the next day, as they were just getting ready to settle into what would now be their seventh bivouac, a helicopter landed on the summit of the Half Dome. They were rescued in the dark of night by Robbins, who abseiled 300m to get the men out of their precarious situation. Despite all their differences in opinion over the years, these two strong characters of the Golden Age never held a personal grudge. As people, Robbins and Harding respected one another. It was natural that Robbins would spring into action immediately in such an emergency as this.

By 1968, four years had gone by since the first ascent of North America Wall. Four years in which Robbins had been away in Europe and involved in other areas. He had done all the big wall routes, either first or second ascents. All except the Muir Wall. In April he made the second ascent, in ten days, and solo:

> 'There are no *reasonable* reasons why one solos. I have done solo climbs because I *had* to do them. I was driven by an unrelenting demon inside, and that demon is difficult to assuage, he always asks for more, more, more. He never gets enough. He is insatiable, gluttonous, ever lusting for more of that particular meat on which he feeds.'[7]

After a few years away here was Robbins back again, in full swing. He wanted more, climbing harder than ever. The new project he had in mind was the very blank central part of Half Dome's North-West Face. None of his usual partners were around at the time, so he chose Don Peterson, a young climber from Colorado. But the days they spent on the wall became a disaster of personal relationships. In a marvellous article that Robbins later wrote about the climb (Tis-sa-ack – A4/5.9 now A3/5.9) he assumed the persona of both climbers. In this account their different attitudes became clear at an early stage and they were then stuck on the same wall together for days, barely speaking. The rock was so devoid of cracks that they repeatedly had to place bolts and in the end used 110 in what became a drilling nightmare for both of them. In TM Herbert's opinion there were far too many and when it came to climbing ethics he was merciless: 'Hey Robbins, you'll set a bad example. Pretty soon we'll have guys bolting up blank walls all over the Valley … Robbins you're finished. You're going downhill.'[4]

Despite this, Robbins received little criticism. This was partly because he remained the opinion leader of Camp 4 and partly because during the summer of 1970, Harding and Rowell had themselves used a record 180 bolts in 500m of the South Face of Half Dome (A4/5.8 now A2+/5.8).

These efforts did little to inspire but the real end of the Golden Age was marked by the controversial first and second ascents of the Wall of Early Morning Light (A4/5.8 now A3/5.8) – the tall section of rock between The Nose and North America Wall. Over a period of twenty-seven days in 1970, Harding and Dean Caldwell worked their way up the wall, managing it eventually in one push, without the use of fixed ropes. The climb was significant for the length of time spent on it and the fact that Harding, stung by the criticism of his style on The Nose and Leaning Tower, set out to make an alpine-style ascent; a brilliant achievement, had the small matter of 330 bolts not come in its way. Forty percent of the 900m wall had been bolted. Headlines were already appearing in California newspapers when the two of them had been on the wall for nearly three weeks and rangers mounted a rescue operation. They refused any kind of help with Caldwell's memorable sound-bite: 'A rescue is unwarranted, unwanted and will not be accepted.'[4] Not surprisingly media interest immediately soared. Headlines covered the story daily, helicopters were sent in for photographs of the climbers on the wall and a whole posse of journalists descended on the Valley. As they topped out on 18 November, no less than one dozen television cameras and fifty reporters lay in wait for the two climbers. Harding's iconoclastic response to the usual question of why anyone would do such a thing was 'because we're insane'.[4] The media frenzy went on for a period but Harding and Caldwell soon fell out over who could exploit the photos and the lecture and TV demands. Embittered, Harding made

considered repeating the climb would be deterred from adopting Harding's style. Naturally, Robbins was at the forefront: 'Any idiot could bolt his way up El Capitan.' For him it was all too clear that the mere existence of the route spelt the end of adventure climbing. Two months later he went to repeat the climb with Don Lauria with the intention of removing the bolts. Lauria led on the first pitch and watched rather shocked as Robbins followed taking out all the bolts as he went. 'Royal assured me that if we descended without accomplishing complete erasure, TM Herbert would personally castrate both of us.'[5]

By the end of the day, however, Robbins himself was no longer sure if he was right. Despite all the bolts, the climbing was excellent and very challenging. The bolts were also not as close as they had expected.

> 'That night I lay awake in my hammock thinking about it and I finally decided that I no longer felt right about destroying the route ... So I was faced with this existential problem which I would see quite clearly: should I act for the sake of consistency, which would certainly bring me harsh criticism, or should I stop something I now felt was wrong – and by doing so look like a fool? I decided I had to stop, because if my actions were going to be motivated solely by consideration of what people would think, I was finished anyway.'[5]

The deep rift, which resonated through Camp 4 after the Wall of Early Morning Light affair, marked the end of an era. In the short span of fifteen years, a bunch of young enthusiasts and powerful personalities had not only revolutionised climbing in Yosemite but the world over.

one last statement and withdrew from the climbing scene completely. 'This whole affair has caused me anguish, disillusionment and bitterness, but now I am only weary of it and would like nothing better than to forget it.'[4]

Many of the Valley climbers were critical of both the climb and the media circus, and it was not long before they openly discussed removing all the bolts and eliminating the route. That way, anyone who

References: 7 *American Alpine Journal*; 4 *Camp 4*; 5 *Defying Gravity*

11 THE FREE-CLIMBING REVOLUTION

Just as the 1960s were synonymous with big wall climbing, the 1970s were with free climbing. This was not just true of Yosemite but all over the United States. The pursuit of hard free climbing (plus the appearance of the cordless drill in the 1980s) eventually led some climbers to adopt sport climbing, as we know it today. Although Sacherer and Pratt had already been successful free climbers and indeed Robbins, Kor and others were also very skilled, it was now up to the next generation of climbers to make free climbing the prevailing discipline in Yosemite.

Jim "The Bird" Bridwell stood at the centre of the new generation. He had already experienced the world of climbing in Yosemite as a teenager in 1962. During the next nine years he had climbed most of the important routes in the Valley. He was the link, as it were, between the Golden Age climbers and the young new recruits and adopted the same role that Robbins once held.

According to John Long:

> 'Jim Bridwell was the de-facto Lord of Camp 4 and everyone in it. He had a vulpine smile and a gymnast's frame and was the biggest name in American climbing. He was just enough older than us that he seemed to know everything. In a manner a rope ran from Jim back to the very beginning of the sport …'[9]

In addition, he climbed with all the great legends: Layton Kor, Royal Robbins, Allen Steck, Chuck Wilts, Norman Clyde. He also nurtured that link with the younger climbers. He would take one after the other up some of the best routes at the time. New Dimensions (A0/5.10) on the Arch Rock with Mark Klemens, Hot Line (A0/5.10b) on Elephant Rock with Mark Chapman, the Crucifix (A1/5.10c) on the Higher Cathedral Rock with Kevin Worrall (the aid here usually indicating tension traverses to link cracks). In 1971, "Lord Bridwell" himself set his own personal record with the ascent of Nabisco Wall (5.11a). His pupils, meanwhile, were soon known as the finest free climbers in the world, tackling some of the toughest routes in the world: La Escuela (5.11b) a three-pitch route on El Capitan by Mark Chapman and Steve Wunsch, the Bircheff/Williams (5.11b) on Middle Cathedral Rock by Kevin Worrall and George Meyers.

The number of climbers in the Valley grew, not only due to the free-climbing trend but because young climbers were fascinated with and attracted to the lifestyle. True to the times, the community in Camp 4 developed into a hippie subculture. Weed was widespread and soon smoking grass was the second most important thing in Camp 4 life. It did not stop at soft drugs though. LSD, peyote and mescaline – they experimented with them all. It is no myth that some were so high when climbing even the big walls that they had no idea what was going on. Drugs weren't necessarily conducive to getting up early and tackling tough routes however. Easy going and hangin' out were the themes of this new lifestyle.

> 'Throughout the 1970s,' John Long wrote,[9] 'Camp 4 was emblematic for all that was illegitimate, including everyone who lived there. Entire summers would pass without seeing a single ranger. They had better things to do than prowl through a ghetto of bohemians who made a career out of climbing rocks and wasting time. The place had been written off as some sort of leper colony.' Camp 4 was like a big family. 'Furthermore, sex, and plenty of it, was an

indispensable aspect of our training routine. According to the Bird, perilous climbs demanded steadiness and a zen-like acuity impossible to achieve when freighted with 'urgent fluids'. They encumbered the Astral Body. The fluids had to go.'[7]

They were extremely creative in their nighttime search for liberation. Following nature's example, their tents were transformed into love nests. The largest of these was of course that of Lord Bridwell.

Early in 1977, a blessing came to the Camp 4 residents from upon high. A plane full to the brim with marijuana had crashed into a frozen lake just thirty kilometres away in the Sierra Nevada. It was soon clear that there was enough there to make everyone in camp very rich. Bridwell was away in Patagonia but his group were energised into making a long winter hike through the snows to the crash site. They soon came back each carrying fifty kilograms of grass with a value of at least $50,000.

'"Hiking for Dollars" we called it and in a week's time more than half a million dollars worth of booty had been hauled to light. Climbers who a few weeks before hadn't got two dimes to rub together, streamed back into the Valley and were spending cash with all the nonchalance of a Saudi prince ...'[9]

Of course their riches did not last long and the climbers soon found themselves back in their beloved Camp 4. Wealth and material gain were still only abstract values to them. "Living in the dirt" was the phrase coined to describe the way they lived at that time, and a pretty accurate one it seems!

The first free-climbing surprise came in the spring of 1973 with the arrival of Henry Barber. This climber from the east coast showed the residents what free climbing was really about. Barber was different from the others. Instead of cracking open a beer to celebrate the end of a climb, he would carry on climbing as many routes as he could in a day. Barber's masterpiece took place on Cookie Cliff. For some time a thin finger crack up the wall above Wheat Thin had been stopping some powerful attempts. After an initial fall, Barber succeeded in climbing it on his second attempt naming it Butterballs (5.11c). He had thus captured Yosemite's toughest crack ... a notable coup. As is often the case, success attracted jealousy and resentment. Jim Bridwell recorded the reaction at the time:

The climbers in Yosemite at the time were kind of lolly-gagging around, so Henry went off and bagged some real gems. And that pissed some people off. I remember one time he and [Steve] Wunsch were hitchhiking back to the Valley from some climb, and Steve says to Henry 'Hey, why don't you go hide down there in the bushes. We'll have a better chance of getting picked up if people don't see you.' That shows how popular Henry was in the Valley.[7]

The absolute refusal to use pitons in free climbing was representative of this era of climbing. By the mid-1960s, the first "nuts" reached Yosemite. The Brits had been using chockstones since the 1920s. Small round pebbles, jammed into cracks and used as aids. By the 1950s they had supplanted them with reamed engine nuts threaded by a sling, and in the early 1960s simple alloy chocks and wedges appeared. Since hammering in pitons left scars on the cracks in Yosemite, these new wedges meant no traces would be left on the rock. Robbins was the first to use some of these early

British nuts in Yosemite, but it was not until Chouinard and Frost began to manufacture and market them in the United States in the early 1970s that they really took off thus allowing the "clean climbing" ethos to develop.

One peculiarity of the time was that hang dogging (checking out the moves of a route while hanging on the rope) was seen as cheating. This made gathering information about routes far more complex. Whereas today's sport climbers, protected by pre-placed bolts, have little else to think of except how they are to make their next move, on traditional climbs protection has to be placed, and secured, as one progresses. In the early 1970s, before the appearance of good wired nuts and friends, this process was more difficult – particularly on steep climbs. Decisions had to be made how often to place protection, how reliable it was, and where the next protection place might be. Climbing in this way was always a tussle between dwindling power reserves and the will to complete the route successfully. However, one thing was guaranteed, and that was that as soon as you fell, you would be lowered to the ground to begin from the start.

The local's anti-hero, "Hot Henry" Barber, came back to the Valley in 1975. He could not of course leave again without setting one more milestone. His ascent of Fish Crack (5.12b) in the Cascade area was the first 5.12 route done in Yosemite!

1975 turned out to be an exceptionally productive year. The simple reason was that the free-climbing fraternity in Camp 4 was growing. The new climbers who were steadily improving their skills were now poised to produce results. The best of the bunch were Ron Kauk and John Bachar. The pair made a formidable team, leaving their mark on the free-climbing scene throughout the 1970s. Together with

John Long, they free climbed all of the steep, overhanging, granite pitches of Astroman (5.11c). These were clean, clear cracks. It was varied climbing at its best and very demanding. In achieving this *team-free-ascent* (i.e. sharing the leads) of Harding's Washington Column route, they had transformed it into one of the world's most brilliant climbs.

Just a few months later, Kauk even managed a redpoint ascent of Astroman in just one day! In Kauk and Bachar, the free-climbing revolution had found its two leading figures. Their most celebrated achievement happened in 1978, right in the middle of Camp 4 on the Columbia Boulder. For twenty years, camp life had centred itself round this huge lump of rock. People had partied round the campfire there, slept there, met there and prepared themselves for big wall routes by it. One of the strongest climbers was John Yablonski who came from the Joshua Tree area of southern California. He believed the four-metre overhanging east side of the boulder was climbable. Kauk and Bachar worked on the problem for four months until, after numerous attempts, Kauk was first to complete it.

Over the years, Midnight Lightning (Fb7b+) became the most widely known boulder problem in the Valley. The contribution John Bachar made to its reputation, as a close second behind Kauk, was certainly not insignificant. For a long time, Kauk and Bachar were the only ones who could climb Midnight Lightning. As soon as other climbers attempted the problem, Bachar would appear from nowhere and complete it with such playful ease that most climbers immediately beat a hasty and frustrated retreat. Bachar was also quick to exploit Midnight Lightning's potential to improve his life in Camp 4. He who wanted a photograph of him on the boulder would have to pay up.

A feat carried out by Ron Kauk one year earlier also grew to be just as renowned. Separate Reality in the Cascade Falls area, at 5.11d was by no means a landmark itself at the time. As a seven-metre roof, however, its completion marked the huge progress being made in free climbing for the image of climbers on such a ceiling was sensational. Overhangs like this were still being surmounted with the use of etriers in Europe, but here in America they were now being climbed free!

One would have expected that it would be one of these two climbers who took that magical next step to a 5.13 grade climb. Looking at it now, the two certainly had it in them to do it but it was actually Ray Jardine who made that step. Jardine had nowhere near the climbing skills of either Kauk or Bachar but had a similar attitude to Harding. He did not care what others thought and was prepared to try his hand at anything that could help push his limits further. At that time any climber to take a fall would, in accordance with Camp 4 ethics, immediately be lowered and have to start again from the ground. By this method, it was extremely difficult to crack the crux moves on a 5.13 route. Jardine ignored this rule, and it was not long before his "hang dogging" tactic was universally adopted. 'I climbed as high as I could and then lay back on the rope to shake my arms. I then carried on climbing free, not using any of the aid for my moves. I called it "working" a route as I think it is still called today.'[7]

Jardine thus had an advantage as he could hang on the rope and study crux moves. In 1976 and 1977 he had a whole series of tough routes to his name, with catchy titles such as Crimson Cringe (5.12a), Hang Dog Flyer (5.12c), Rostrum Roof (5.12b) and Elephant's Eliminate (5.12d). His successful spell peaked in June 1977. He spotted a forty-metre overhanging crack opposite the

Rostrum. 'The first time I saw the crack of Phoenix, I knew that it was part of another dimension when it came to difficulty. 'He carefully practised his "hang dogging" style on it and eventually led what was probably the world's first 5.13 route. The judgement he received from Camp 4 was negative and critical. According to the strict ethics his Phoenix ascent was nothing short of deceitful. Jardine had a tendency to not mention key facts. An example of this was the first ascent of Crimson Cringe where he omitted to note that he had done the forty-metre crack in three rope lengths. Such lack of candour and general secretiveness meant that none of his achievements were acclaimed by any of Camp 4's leading climbers.

A key factor in Jardine's exceptional string of successes was his great invention – the Friend – a camming device that fitted into cracks. Jardine was an aerospace engineer and therefore fully versed in metallurgy and machine tool design. His prototypes of the Friend came in four sizes allowing it to fit snugly into Yosemite's parallel-sided cracks of widths from 2cms to 10cms. The confidence engendered on these hard climbs by having such easy-to-place protection was immense. His early repeat of Separate Reality, for example, was straightforward whereas Kauk had initially tried to protect it with a long sling hung down the crack from above. When that didn't work he resorted to a series of nut placements strenuously fixed from below during several attempts (and left in place for other repeats of the climb). It was the widely circulated photo of Jardine repeating this route with Friends after these nuts had been removed that established its fame.

Jardine had offered his Friend design to various American manufacturers, but eventually linked up with the English climber/entrepreneur Mark Vallance who solved the mass production difficulties. The first commercial models appeared in the shops in January

1978 and, though expensive, were soon recognised as an important advance. Crack climbing difficulties were greatly eased by their use for both aid and protection. These far-reaching influences were barely recognised at the time and Yosemite climbers were merely enraged by Jardine's climbing tactics. In the early 1970s the brave new world of free climbing beckoned but the end of the decade saw the Valley, yet again, embroiled in controversy, exactly as it had been with Robbins and Harding a decade earlier. This simmered throughout the 1980s. Even when Bill Price carried out the first ascent of Cosmic Debris (5.13b) in 1980 and the Englishman Jerry Moffatt managed an on-sight ascent of the Phoenix, proving that climbing had progressed, the mood in the Valley concerning sport climbing was still very unenthusiastic. It is not surprising that the 1970s free-climbing boom, that had started so well, became curiously eclipsed by the sport-climbing craze that was soon to gain pace elsewhere.

The next development came with the return of Ron Kauk after a few years away climbing in world competitions. From his knowledge of European climbing he advanced new ideas. 'I've always been open to further development in the sport. I also believe that bolts could revive the stagnating scene in Yosemite and free climbing could carry on.'** But the traditional, conservative core in Camp 4 would have nothing to do with it and were furious about bolted sport climbs with John Bachar at the front of this backlash. Kauk's group believed the only way to keep up with the Europeans in sport climbing was by drilling bolts from an abseil/rappel rope (rap-bolting). Bachar's camp on the other hand was not interested in European attitudes and the grades of difficulty being achieved. For them, climbing was not just a sport but also an adventure.

'The fact is that Yosemite produces some of the hardest ground-up routes in the world to date

and the standards are increasing every year. Only because top-down routes are equated with traditional ground-up routes, via the usage of the same numeric rating system, do Yosemite-style ground-up first ascents appear inferior. After all what is harder, doing an on-sight, on-the-lead first ascent of a 5.13b, or doing a top-down, rehearsed, preprotected 5.14a? They are two different games, born of opposite approaches and producing different results. The climbing in Yosemite and its traditions deserve to be respected.'[5]

With this attitude, Bachar went on to open up routes that even the world's top climbers like Jerry Moffatt and Wolfgang Güllich had shied away from. You Asked For It (5.10c) and the famous Bachar/Yerian (5.11c) on Medlicott Dome in the Tuolumne Meadows were two examples which were not of extreme difficulty but bold. Bachar had done both of these as first ascents in 1980, ground-up, with minimal use of protection bolts.

With the help of skyhooks on the Bachar/Yerian, he placed a total of just three bolts over the forty metres of the crux pitch. Quite a few aspiring climbers would bury any thought of returning to a climb after having a big fall. Even more of them would quit after taking one look at what they were meant to climb.

Throughout all the debates, both sides were incredibly stubborn. The compromise between the two, which is so often the best solution to such a situation, was never reached. For a while, the fight was out in the open. Bachar carried on opening up first ascents in the traditional style, whilst Kauk retorted with routes that were rap-bolted such as European Vacation (5.13b). When Kauk completed a route in his style that Bachar had started 'ground-up' but not finished, provocatively named Peace (5.12d), the war of traditions sharpened. But Bachar, now weary of the arguments, withdrew from the Yosemite climbing scene. Without its greatest supporter, the traditionalist camp lost some of its energy.

Nevertheless Yosemite has never developed as a sport-climbing area. Even when Kauk opened up tough new routes such as Crossroads (5.13d) in 1993 and Magic Line (5.14b) in 1997, the fact still remained that often featureless granite in Yosemite just wasn't suited to a large number of top-grade sport routes. This is because most of its walls do not offer enough holds to make rap-bolted sport climbing worthwhile. Even today Yosemite is essentially a place for traditional climbing.

* From 'Back Then', *Rock and Ice* magazine 19??.
** From *Rock Stars* by Heinz Zak (Rudolf Rother, Munich 1995).

Left: The wide black waterstreak on the West Face of Medlicott Dome, Tuolumne, forms an ideal natural topo for the Bachar/Yerian route (5.11c)

GOLF BALLS FROM HEAVEN

In the late 1970s, two of the residents of Camp 4 decided they would practise their swing on the El Cap Towers, half-way up El Capitan. Equipped with full golf sets and about two hundred stolen golf balls, they climbed over The Nose in search of their chosen tee spot. They then spent a lovely afternoon, launching golf balls way down into the El Cap Meadows. John Long recalls:

'Several cars were struck, windshields shattered. The rangers closed the road down for three hours and fanned out on horseback looking for a sniper. Cars backed up, overheated, rammed each other and tourists fought. There were several arrests. The case was never solved.'

Golf balls of granite on Lambert Dome

The Dike Route (5.9) on Pywiack Dome, Tuolumne

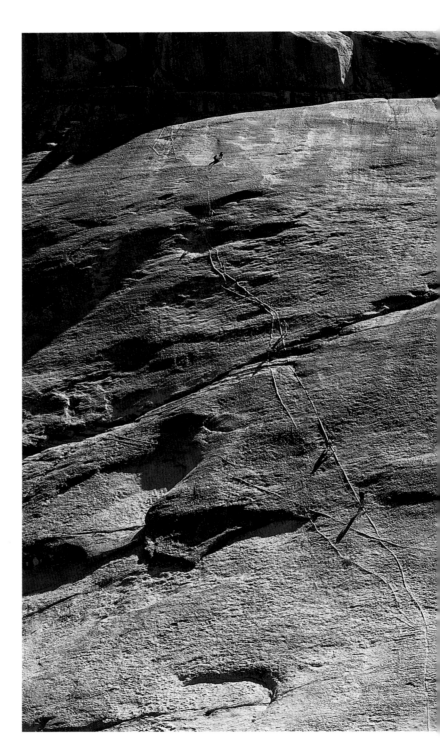

Jim Bridwell

12 Brave New World

The general concept of climbing in Yosemite is centred on the mystique of big walls. However, the glorious sweeping plains of sunlit granite that capture the imagination of the primary climbing urge have lost their lustrous aura. Advancements in equipment and, more precisely, in knowledge have stripped the mystery shrouding the big walls, laying bare the boring and laborious logistics and the stifling repetition and tedium of placing one gadget after another into begrudging cracks.

In more recent years an ever-growing vanguard of imaginative and progressive young climbers has been fostering a fast-moving renaissance of Yosemite free climbing. Refined techniques, strength training, equipment improvement and purification of ethics have led to amazing new routes. Yesterday's aid climb is today's standard free climb. The pressure of the ever-evolving spirit within has started to be felt and is now expressing itself in the idealism of imaginative new routes, in the beauty of control of mind, and the precision of movement which is required for the execution of these routes.

Originally, free climbing in Yosemite was not as important as aid-climbing technology, for the major walls were unclimbed. The evolution of climbing marched onward to the first prize and, once the walls were mastered, the goal moved on toward refinement. Free climbing was primarily a display of virtuosity. A master of free climbing was not held captive by the ball and chain of mechanical reliance. The urge was to excel and consequently free climbing began to evolve.

What could be more exhilarating than climbing steep rock uninhibited by aid gadgetry? Bouldering developed as a separate pastime with its own unique challenges. Some climbers stopped climbing and took up bouldering exclusively, while others used it to develop techniques for harder free climbing.

Ethics started to change, ideas and attitudes underwent reconsideration. More and more possibilities were opened. At this stage the hydra of ethics and style began to show its many heads. Fine points normally overlooked assumed importance. The scruples of a first ascent have always been met either with criticism or praise, and unwritten laws have gradually been formulated over the years.

At present styles and ethics have become homogenised into spartan austerities. The new ideals have left certain free-climbing ethics *passé*. All-nut ascents and 'flashing' a route are more desirable than using pitons and sieging a pitch yo-yo style. Today, few climbs, big walls excepted, are done initially as aid climbs. New ethics now regard top-roping, or placing protection on rappels, as highly undesirable.

Unfortunately these styles and ethics form the basis of insidious competition which can prove quite abrasive to the psyche of the climbing community. Ethics and aesthetics are an important feature of this development, and *vice versa*. As new vistas are open, changes will inevitably occur. We may frown at the ideas of the new generation, but they are likely to become selectively assimilated as part of the future norm. The decisions to be made in this respect will be the responsibility of the new generation. These decisions will direct the future of the art and determine whether or not it is to remain an art.

The form of free climbing is defined, the refinement infinite. The seeds are already sprouting in many devoted practitioners of the art. Speculations are

many and varied, but the future definitely holds exciting possibilities. The unusual situation presented by Yosemite has developed a unique life. The concentrated, difficult climbing and the easy-living environment are conducive to long periods of staying in the Valley. All this has given rise to an attitude of mind that believes nothing to be impossible, and has made Yosemite a climber's Utopia: the Mecca of Rock Climbing.

*Bob Boorman on Twilight Zone
(5.10d), Cookie Cliff*

Mark Chapman

13 TIME CAPSULE

Considering its current popularity and historical significance, it's hard to imagine that when I first visited Yosemite as a young climber of sixteen it was virtually unknown outside of America. The year was 1971 and climbing was my passion. I was not alone. In Yosemite I found others who shared my disease. Climbing wasn't nearly the socially accepted activity it is today. In the eyes of the establishment, climbers were considered oddballs, or worse – sociopaths. Indeed, their lifestyle must have seemed strange to the uninitiated, often giving up jobs and careers just to move to Yosemite and climb. I am reminded of the quote of onetime Yosemite climber Eric Beck who noted that 'at either end of the social spectrum lies a leisured class.'

These early climbers, however, were anything but leisurely. The product of their energies would go on to influence countless others to follow in their footsteps, and in the process turn climbing into a mainstream sport.

Yosemite climbing, at that time, was still dominated by the accomplishments of climbers from the 1960s whose ascents of Yosemite's great walls first brought it to the attention of the outside world. Just as big wall climbing dominated the 1960s, free climbing not just in Yosemite but all across America dominated the 1970s, laying the foundation for the sport as we know it today. With most of the major walls and geological formations having been climbed, the new generation turned to smaller more obscure formations on which to leave their mark.

Arch Rock, the Cookie Cliff and Reed's Pinnacle were the new arena. Climbers put aside the cumbersome aid style of the previous generation. Armed with chalk, EBs – the forerunner the modern climbing shoes, and the new hexcentrics – a superior type of nut that

excelled in protecting Yosemite's parallel sided cracks, they soon established a dramatic rise of standards. Boldness and "clean climbing" – the minimal use of rock-damaging bolts and pitons – was the new ethic. The Golden Age of Yosemite free climbing was born.

And what a grand time it was! A wonderland of surrealistic cracks and towering faces just begging to be climbed. The energy was contagious as every spring the best climbers in the world were drawn together with one common goal – climbing. It was a free and easy lifestyle in the most awe-inspiring setting imaginable, a time when bonds were formed that would become enduring friendships, and the routes climbed become part of history. This was the Yosemite that would become immortalised in George Meyers's classic book *Yosemite Climber* that put Yosemite in the hearts and minds of climbers the world over.

Of all the great climbers of this era two rose to the top – Ron Kauk and John Bachar. At first friends drawn together by their talent and love of climbing, they teamed up to create Yosemite's first 5.12 with their free ascent of Hot Line in 1975. Later they would become ideological enemies, each with a different vision of Yosemite's future.

Kauk, a gifted boulderer, personified the Yosemite climber of Meyers's book. Upon his arrival in Yosemite he immediately climbed the hardest routes, and in the next few years would establish some of Yosemite's most memorable free routes.

Bachar's rise to the top was as dramatic as Kauk's. Though not quite as naturally a gifted climber as Kauk, he was extremely driven to be the best and trained religiously. Bachar and Kauk raised the level of difficulty into the 5.12 range, but that in itself is deceptive. Had they used the techniques that were to follow both were fully capable of climbing 5.13.

The enigmatic Ray Jardine, inventor of Friends (which would radically alter the relative difficulty of most crack climbs), was the first to climb 5.13 in Yosemite. However, this was accompanied by a marked compromise in style – hang dogging. Whether viewed as heretic or visionary, Jardine, and the methods he employed, were harbingers of the ethical debates that were to follow.

The 1980s represented the dark ages of Yosemite climbing. As the well of traditional-style new routes began to dry up, and the once close Camp 4 community disbanded, the energy and vibrancy disappeared with it. While standards rose and techniques evolved in other climbing areas, the Yosemite scene stagnated. Foreign climbers visiting Yosemite expecting the promised land depicted in *Yosemite Climber* were disappointed, finding instead an unmotivated, negative environment. Many were treated rudely by locals. Yosemite, justifiably, began to receive a great deal of bad press. At the heart of this turmoil stood, ironically, John Bachar.

With Kauk's absence, Bachar stood unchallenged at the top of the Yosemite climbing hierarchy. He exerted a tremendous influence over Yosemite's young climbers, and the scene reflected his style and personality. Bachar viewed outside climbers, and sport climbing in particular, as a threat to his position and ideals. The very climbers that Bachar once inspired with his climbing were now being alienated by his personality.

The one bright spot of the 1980s was the emergence of Canadian climber Peter Croft. The unassuming

Mark Chapman on Moby Dick Ahab (5.10b),
El Capitan Base

Croft, with his strong sense of climbing history and tradition, had been quietly amassing an impressive catalogue of ascents when, in 1987, he stunned the Valley climbing scene with his amazing free solo of Astroman on Washington Column. Croft, more than any other, epitomised the classic Yosemite climber in the modern era.

By the mid-1980s the situation had deteriorated. There were increasingly ugly confrontations between locals and foreign climbers. It was the only time I truly felt embarrassed to be a Yosemite climber. The time had come to turn the page.

Things came to a head in 1987. The previous year Kauk had been invited to a climbing competition in Europe. He arrived in the land of sport climbing equipped with cut-off jeans and an old-style swami belt. He received a warm reception and climbed well. Intrigued by the new style, and impressed with the level of climbing by the sport's new stars, he returned to Yosemite with open eyes. The following year he created a rap-bolted route, Punchline, at Arch Rock.

Bachar immediately chopped the bolts. A few days later a brief but heated altercation took place in the Camp 4 parking lot. A punch was thrown. Bachar collapsed in the dust of the hallowed grounds of Camp 4 and with him fell the last obstacle to modern climbing in Yosemite.

*Peter Janschek jumaring with haulbags
on the Shield (A2+), El Capitan*

14 AID CLIMBING EVOLVES

Although aided big wall climbing did not capture the headlines in the years after the Golden Age there had still been many developments in this area. The ethics surrounding big wall ascents were just as strict as those surrounding free climbing. Royal Robbins's example was fervently followed.

The first progressive step was made on El Capitan. In 1972 Jim Dunn soloed a new route called Cosmos (A3+/5.8) between the Salathé and Dihedral Walls. Such an achievement would surely have been applauded by Robbins – a new big wall route done solo being the only feat he did not achieve.

Next to make his mark was Charlie Porter. Unlike most in the Valley, Porter was not drawn away from big wall climbing by the developments in free climbing. The 1960s had brought about such high standards in the big wall field that huge advances now seemed unlikely. Yet Porter still managed to fine-tune and perfect the use of artificial aids on his first ascents. The RURP became Porter's favourite tool, which he used like no other. One of his most famous aid climbs was the Shield (A5/5.9 now A2+/5.9) to the left of the upper parts of Muir Wall and The Nose. No other aid route inspires climbers more. It provides seven steeply overhanging pitches up a convex bulge of featureless granite. Just watching aid climbers at work on the climb fills an onlooker with a sense of despair. They seem lost, marooned in the middle of nowhere, more than on any other face of El Capitan. With binoculars, one can follow their moves, and only then detect the thin triple cracks that allow progress. Against a deep blue Californian sky, with the use of only forty RURPs, Porter climbed his way to create one of the most impressive climbs in the world.

In the autumn of 1972, Porter established another all-

time classic with Zodiac (A5/5.8 now A2+/5.8), which took the impending precipice right of North America Wall. Nobody had yet climbed this almost continuously overhanging part of El Capitan. Unable to persuade anyone to join him on this project, Porter went at it alone, and succeeded. Unlike the South-West Face, this wall had no series of cracks nor any obvious feature. The 500m wall stretching in front of him would be no walkover. The sixteen pitches of Zodiac, though steep, unfolded in a direct and logical way. These days it is one of the most fashionable of the steeper El Capitan walls.

With eight first ascents on El Capitan in just four years, Porter had added a new dimension to big wall climbing. But it was to be Jim Bridwell, returning to aid climbing, who was to make the next forward move. Bridwell had spotted a crack line up blank cliffs left of North America Wall – perhaps the most striking precipice on El Capitan. After several failed attempts, with the help of Billy Westbay, Fred East and Jay Fiske, he completed the route in May 1975, noting afterwards:

> '… the eighth pitch was really hard … far and away the hardest pitch done at that time. It took four and a half hours to lead the thing. But the climb set a whole new standard for aid climbing. It probably changed me more than any other route. After that I knew no matter how bad things looked that I could still do it.'

They named what was, at that time, perhaps the hardest aid route in the world, Pacific Ocean Wall (A5/5.9 now A3+/5.9), due to its position just left of North America Wall.

Jim Bridwell and Dale Bard however, set the greatest masterpiece of that time with their 1978 ascent of

Sea of Dreams (A5/5.9 now A4/5.9), an even harder route that starts between the Pacific Ocean and North America Walls. The tenth pitch was exceptional. Bridwell started from the Continental Shelf – 'The rule is easy to understand: you either know how to use your hook or you book your ticket to the other side.'

'Hook or Book' thus became the benchmark of really hard aid climbing as it evolved into an ever more psychological challenge. On hard aid you can expect that a mistake would most likely result in a big and possibly painful or fatal fall.

Another event of note took place in the 1970s. Beverly Johnson and Sibylle Hechtel with their ascent of Triple Direct (A2/5.9) in 1973 became the first female team to complete a route up El Capitan. Bev Johnson, one of Yosemite's more vivid personalities, was one of the first women to spend long periods in Camp 4 and approach climbing with the same passion as the men. Amongst her other climbs she made a solo ascent of Dihedral Wall at a time when the men who had done it solo were still an élite few. Sadly Bev Johnson died in a helicopter accident in 1994.

Johnson's ascents put a swift end to all the mutterings of women being better at following men up routes and showed they could be equal partners on a rope. What seems obvious today was not quite clear to the men in Camp 4 during the 1970s.

Coincidentally, about that time, a woman climber joined this male dominated world, who would later revolutionise climbing in the Valley. Her name was Lynn Hill and her first noteworthy ascent was in 1977 when she climbed the Shield with Mari Gingery.

Left: With haulbags on the summit of El Capitan

Below: Jumaring on Tangerine Trip (A2+), El Capitan

Page 92: Wally Barker on the first ascent of Plastic Surgery Disaster (A5–), one of the toughest techno-routes on El Capitan

Page 93: Heinz Zak on the Shield (A2+), El Capitan

91

The 1980s saw the development of an unbelievable number of new aid routes with El Capitan the main focus of attention. Robbins had thought there could only be a maximum of twenty further routes on El Capitan. This decade alone saw thirty new lines being added. Though many were very fine, their sheer number meant that they attracted far less applause than those of earlier times.

One that stood out was Wyoming Sheep Ranch done in 1984. Rob Slater and John Barbella rated this route at A5+ at the time, the hardest grade ever for an aid route on El Capitan but now graded A4/5.8. It became clear that the ceiling of the ratings scale was getting closer. A5 grading had already been given out in the 1960s and 70s to North America Wall and Pacific Ocean Wall. Since then Sea of Dreams (A5/5.9) and Charles Coles's Jolly Roger (A5/5.10) had been downgraded to A4 though they were obviously far harder than the earlier A5s. Locked into their conservative straight jacket of believing that old grading norms must be maintained and that A5 had to form the upper limit, American climbers began to adopt quirky ideas to overcome

this dilemma. On the first ascent of the Big Chill (A4/5.9) on Half Dome, Bridwell and Peter Mayfield made up their own grading system: NBD – no big deal, NTB – not too bad, PDH – pretty darn hard. According to Mayfield, most of their routes came under the PDH section.

These were of course just fickle solutions and would never be seriously accepted. With newer routes presenting greater difficulties and the A5 grade forming an iron ceiling, many of the older routes would have to be lowered a grade or two. "New Wave Grading" was therefore introduced in the 1990s.

Don Reid's guidebook *Big Walls* (1993) began the process giving North America Wall a reduced rating of A3/5.8. The readjustment continued after this and Wyoming Sheep Ranch (1984) which Reid graded A5+ is now graded at A4 new wave (or nw). Mescalito (originally A5 and A4 in Reid) is now considered nwA3. Thus one must take care to find out which grading scale your chosen route is from. Even today most guidebooks do not explain these

Left: Thomas Tivadar on Highway to Hell (A5), El Capitan

nuances of the aid grading system. Any first ascent during the late 1990s will definitely be according to the New Wave grading, and is usually "pretty darn hard" for its grade.

One of the most prolific climbers breaking new ground in the 1990s was Eric Kohl. Most of his first ascents such as Plastic Surgery Disaster (A5/5.8 now A5–) were done solo, illustrating that new climbing gear meant that solo ascents did not really require much more effort than the old method of roped parties. Solo ascents ask for more commitment but the main barrier in the past was psychological. This too has now been largely removed – solo aided ascents are now commonplace.

The most beautiful first ascent of the 1990s had to be Reticent Wall (A5/5.9) by Steve Gerberding, Scott Stowe and Lauri Ridder. The route lies between The Nose and Wall of Early Morning Light, following a set of barely visible thin cracks. It is also the only route that today is accorded the full A5 grade although there is talk of it being reduced to nwA4+. Gerberding continued to demonstrate that he has an instinct for where to find new big wall routes with his 1993 and 1998 ascents of Gulf Stream (nwA4/5.10) with John Harpole and Jay Smith, and Continental Drift (nwA4/5.9) with Kevin Thaw and Conrad Anker.

I had an amazing experience in 1998 watching the German/Hungarian team of Thomas Tivadar and Gabor Berecz on the first ascent of Highway to Hell (nwA5/5.9). They were using bat hooks instead of bolts for protection so the first pitch really tempted fate. The first crack is reached twenty metres up the wall and leading up to that point are only the tiniest edges and all placed above a base slope covered in wild granite boulders. Tivadar made the move from

his last skyhook to the first bird beak, whose thin peak sat half-way in a wafer-thin crack. The closest protection was a small sling around a loose flake about six metres off the ground. Below sat Berecz, calmly staring ahead holding the rope even more calmly. Above, Tivadar was struggling for his life. Watching this was soon too much. I could not look any longer and had to leave. I could even feel the tension as I walked away. My ears were pricked for every sound, waiting for the cry of someone falling and then the inevitable consequences. The cry didn't come. It never came.

That pitch was aptly named The Guillotine and has understandably still not been repeated.

Gabor Berecz on Highway to Hell (A5), El Capitan

Left: Russel Mitrovich, Steph Davis and Beth Coats –
paralysed from the waist down – on Zodiac (A2+)

Right: One of thousands of pull-ups for Beth Coats who,
like Mark Wellman, fulfilled a great ambition

Below: After a portaledge bivouac on the
headwall of the Shield (A2+), El Capitan

FOUR ARMS AND TWO LEGS

A mountain accident left Mark Wellman paralysed from the waist down. After years of rehabilitation, his greatest dream was to carry out an ascent on a big wall.

'If I have learned one thing since my accident, it was that a lot of sweat, determination and positive thinking would allow me to accomplish things that might have seemed impossible. [After the accident] I wanted to face new adversity and challenge, and to live and breathe with it every day until I overcame it. As far as I knew, no paraplegic had even tried to scale any of the big walls in Yosemite, and to me, that made the idea nearly irresistible.'

In 1989, seven years after the accident, Wellman met with Mr. El Cap, Mike Corbett. With over fifty ascents on El Capitan behind him, Corbett was fascinated with Wellman's idea. After three months of preparations and training, they set out for the Shield. As Corbett led the way, Wellman followed on a fixed rope using a block and tackle Jumar system, twelve centimetres at a time, eight pull-ups per metre. Ten thousand pull-ups later, they reached the summit. Wellman fulfilled his dream. 'I knew I would soon be settling back into my wheelchair. I also knew that the person settling in it would never be the same as the one who left it eight days earlier.' Strong will and determination won the day!

A familiar meeting place for Yosemite boulderers – Thriller (Fb7c), Camp 4

Jerry Moffatt

15 BOULDERING

I remember when the book *Yosemite Climber* came out in 1979, it looked so cool, the place to be. Everybody looked tanned with rippled bodies. My heroes like Pete Livesey and Ron Fawcett had been there. I struggled up the 5.8s in the cold in England wearing white trousers and a red headband – probably not looking quite as cool as I thought. I knew I was going to go there one day when I left school. I so wanted to go there, lie about in camp tanning, do a bit of bouldering then perhaps try a desperate crack like Tales of Power.

I spent the winter of 1982 in Joshua Tree and having done the hardest problems headed for the Valley. It snowed for two weeks, nothing got dry and that was the end of that. I'd been away for over six months and I headed back to England.

I returned to the Valley in 1984 and gave Midnight Lightning a try. I got to the lip on the third try but couldn't see what to do. I felt around, shook out and eventually, getting pumped, fell off. Ron Kauk

walked round the corner and immediately showed me the move as he cruised the problem. I got it next go grabbing the fourth ascent. I had fulfilled a dream and was just so happy and excited. I can remember as I reached the finger jug knowing that I had done it. It was just brilliant to repeat such a classic piece of bouldering history.

I periodically returned to the Valley – it's one of my favourite places. But it wasn't until 1992 that I started to add some problems of my own to the established collection. Up to that point the hardest problems were still The Lightning and Thriller, another world-class problem added by Kauk in the mid-1980s. I don't recall just being there to boulder but that's what I ended up doing. I was travelling with Kurt Albert who was also motivated to boulder.

Kauk showed me a new line he had looked at left of Thriller. It started on a small crimpy flake, a difficult cross move and a long move to a layaway initiated a steep wall. The problem is quite high and

the landing bad. It was before crash pads came along so the landing area had to be cleared. Kauk and I spent most of a day moving rocks and getting the landing flat. We went over to the employee's dorms opposite camp and nicked a large wooden pallet. We put this beneath the rock then covered it with mud and pinecones to get it nice and flat.

There was another line I had wanted to try just past Blue Suede Shoes. I had first seen it in 1984. There is an obvious edge on a slab about a metre up above this overhanging boulder, the bottom being too steep to climb. The rock started at head height so I thought if I could just pull on I could slap for the edge. I tried so many methods. Kurt pushed me up to feel various sequences and holds. I kept finding better holds to the right of the line. After a couple of days and a lot of pushing by Kurt, I had a sequence that worked. It starts with two footless moves on real slopers (which looked impossible but worked) followed by a high step. You palm another sloper then slap with either hand for a jug. And that's it. You stood on the slab. Simple but brilliant. I had sussed out both problems but needed a strong day and some good conditions to get them done.

I had a few days off and felt really strong. The temperature was good. I felt confident but nervous. I didn't need much of a warm-up and went straight around to the footless problem. A few explosive pulls and I was stood on the slab. Yes! "Stick It" was born. I just love that problem so much. You could walk past it and never know it was there. Feeling pretty good about myself I put a dip in my hip and a yard in my stride and went to look at the problem left of Thriller.

I must have felt good that day as to my surprise I pulled on and just ripped the first moves. I was at a new high point and into new territory. I remember

101

Below: Two photos of Ron Kauk climbing his master-problem Midnight Lightning (7b+), Camp 4

crossing for a sloper with my right and slapping for a good hold just below the top. Unfortunately, I hadn't cleaned it and it was covered with wet moss. I threw on a heel hook, which slipped straight off. Losing it, my legs began to shake. I was out of control and not looking forward to the fall. I focused on the top and threw for it. Luckily I struck it and I grabbed the top. I called it "The Force" after Michael Jackson's song, which has the first lines 'The force it's got a lot of power'. I felt so happy to have added two problems of my own to those already in the Valley – taking part in the history of one of the foremost climbing areas in the world. I clearly remember thinking; it's worth training your whole life just to have accomplished a couple of problems like these.

I had my eye on another line to the right of Stick It: a forty-five-degree wall of smooth marble-like granite, with a pinch and a couple of small edges on it. Years

before I saw some chalk on the pinch. Dream on I thought to myself. Now it was looking more possible. The landing again wasn't good so I went about repairing it by building it up with blocks and dirt. I was warming up the next day on the classic Blue Suede Shoes. My foot started to slide in the greasy

*Max Reichel on Superdynamo
on a boulder in Camp 4*

conditions as I manteled on a tiny finger edge. I wasn't going to fall off this. I was pressing extra hard on the edge when I heard a crack. Ooh, that was painful. I'd done the problem but damaged a capsule in a finger joint in the process. My finger swelled up and I didn't manage to climb for two months.

I returned again in 1993, again with Kurt Albert, with big plans. We had brought a ton of gear with us, miles of static line in the hope of trying to free The Nose. That quickly went on the back burner. Not being big wall guys, we got distracted by the Camp 4 boulders yet again. I had a look at the overhanging project and Kurt pushed me through the moves. I could nearly hang the holds and if that's possible surely it's possible to move through them. I knew it would go. This is sometimes the best experience of finding something new and that was no exception. I just couldn't stop thinking about it.

The problem goes: pinch right hand – dyno left to an edge – hold the swing (crux) – place right foot – reach an edge with right hand – then slap the top and match. First, there was no point in trying the first move which looked the hardest. So I started working the other moves. It took two days to link it to the top without the first move – I figured it out but it just felt desperate. I couldn't imagine linking it with the first move even if I could do it. The only way to get that quick was to rest and diet. I had a couple of days off and tried not to eat much. I went on a hike up the falls trail which takes about four hours. I did it as

quickly as I could. I ate a small dinner of salad hoping that I might feel good the next day. I even remember sticking a block of chalk in the microwave for ten minutes in the hope it would give a little more grip. I wanted it so bad.

Next morning I pulled on the rock to warm up and just felt bionic. This has got to be the day I thought. I didn't really need to warm up too much as I felt as light as a feather. I went straight to the first move grabbing the pinch and jumping for the edge. I felt good but fumbled the edge – you have to hit it very precisely. I did this a couple more times. I sat on the ground trying to figure out how I could hit the hold right in the middle. If it was a pocket I am sure I would get it right. I got some tape out, ripping bits off and sticking them around the edge to make it look like a pocket.

I shook out and tried to be relaxed and smooth. I pulled and hit the edge perfectly and before I knew it I was slapping the top, holding for the final swing and yes, I had done it! It's impossible to describe the

feeling you get doing something so short and intense. One minute you're sitting thinking will I ever get it and seconds later you make your dream into a reality. The rush of excitement and adrenaline is so intense.

I love the fact the problem is right in camp and so accessible for people to try. There doesn't seem much point in doing something nobody is going to try. I would ideally like all climbers to experience this problem. That night while thinking of a name I typed into Kauk's pocket digital thesaurus the word power. It came up with a few alternatives one of which was dominate, hence the name Dominator as it's just power.

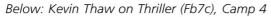

Below: Kevin Thaw on Thriller (Fb7c), Camp 4

Far left and Left: Cedar Wright battling with his crack problem Cedar Eater

Lower left: Rick Cashner on King Boulder, Cathedral Boulders

Below: Rob Miller on Cocain Corner (5.11), Camp 4

106

Left: Billy Westbay, Jim Bridwell and John Long after the first one-day ascent of The Nose of El Capitan (behind)

Tim O'Neill using his skyhook on The Nose

16 SPEED

At first glance, Yosemite is enormous, but over the years the scale of its walls became less daunting. The early focus was to climb all the big walls of the Valley, most of which involved expeditions of several days. After the main objectives had been climbed the evolution became more complex. Today, most big walls are still done over a period of days but the performance-obsessed climbing élite seek to do them in the quickest possible time with as much free climbing as possible.

Speed means that time, that crystal-clear, physical gauge becomes the judge. On your marks, get set and go: the stopwatch measuring every second of every hour, all the way to the very top. Speed is the style that transformed climbers into vertical athletes.

Even the big walls that had first been expeditions of one week, and later a matter of days, were now being done in hours. This incredible reduction in times is the product of a long learning curve, stretching back to the Golden Age.

Although previous years had seen climbers attempt to repeat routes quickly, it was in 1961 that the competition really began. Or as Chouinard put it:

'Climbers climb not just to see how much faster and more efficient they are than a party which did the same climb a few days before. The climb becomes secondary, no more important than a racetrack.'[4]

Steve Roper was the self-confessed leader of this new competitive streak taking hold of Camp 4 where the question, 'How long did you take?' was now the most important concern.

In 1961, exactly one year after Royal Robbins and

Joe Fitschen became the first to climb the Steck/Salathé in a day, Frank Sacherer and Steve Roper knocked ninety minutes off their time. When the two came back to camp they were greeted by Robbins with a bottle of champagne. Robbins showed himself to be truly sporting and open but he could not let this go unchallenged. Speed, the competition against the clock, had started. Robbins held off for one day and then made his try with Tom Frost. For the first time in Yosemite they climbed together (simul-climbing) at the same time without stopping at belay points. They not only broke the record but shattered it by three hours and fifteen minutes. Even more notable however, was Henry Barber's lightning ascent of the Sentinel. He could not find a partner so he just went and climbed the Steck/Salathé solo in just two hours forty-five minutes. In the twenty years since its first ascent, what had been a five-day affair, was now reduced to an afternoon's outing.

Until 1975, El Capitan still provided the necessary challenge. Fifteen years after the first ascent climbers on The Nose were no longer a rarity and the idea of doing this thirty-four-pitch climb in a day was born. As Sacherer had speculated the key to success lay in free climbing because it has the potential to be quicker. This remained merely an idea until, ten years later, Bridwell formulated his plan for 'The Nose in a Day'.

John Long

17 LONG, HARD AND FIRST

In the mid-1970s, the Yosemite climber thought himself king of the heap and nothing pleased us more than to prove it.

At the end of the 1974 season, Jim Bridwell declared that the next year I'd be joining him and Billy Westbay to climb The Nose in one day. At that time, when Lord Jim had big plans we all tried to get in on the action because it was our ticket to glory, meaning we could brag about the accomplishment to the twenty or so people on earth who cared. Anyway, here was my chance to do something great on what we considered the greatest of all rocks, something suited to my restless drive. The Nose in a day became my mantra throughout the school year. Nine months later, I returned to the Valley breathing fire. We started at four in the morning on Labor Day, 1975. Bridwell knew that history would consider our ascent tainted if we used so much as one fixed rope, so to lay claim to a genuine one-day ascent we'd have to climb the whole McGilla, bottom to top, from the ground.

We divided the route into three parts, each one leading the section best suited to his talents. My job was to crank off the initial free pitches to the top of Boot Flake. At six-foot, two, 205 pounds, I had the wrong physique for extreme free climbing, but the initial crack pitches on The Nose – mostly hand and fist cracks – fitted my mitts perfectly.

Never, before or after, did I feel so invincible than when I was powering up those initial crack pitches. Pitch after pitch fell beneath us. Rarely did I place more than one or two nuts per pitch.

Jim and Billy blazed up behind me on jumars, arriving at the belay before I even had time to rack for the next lead. Often throughout my previous five years of climbing I'd exasperated my partners by staying at the cliff long enough to do just one more crack, and how that drill was paying off. My life was reduced to one goal: reaching the next belay. We cooked up the Stovelegs in less than an hour. Just after 7 a.m. I jammed up to the top of Boot Flake, clipped off the anchor and kissed the rock. Billy took over.

In the classic Yosemite tradition, Billy Westbay was the quintessential all-round climber, the kind who vanished twenty years ago: superb on thin cracks, off-widths, flares, runout face climbing, dynamic bouldering or extreme aid. Climbing mixed-style, Billy got us up to Camp 5, some eighty percent up the wall, just after noon. Then Bridwell swung into the lead.

While Billy and I had been climbing like crazy for weeks prior to our one-day attempt, Bridwell had been rounding into shape in San Diego, shooting pool and drinking beer, but spent little if any time on the rock. The Nose in a day was his first real climb since leaving for San Diego a month before. No one but Bridwell – then or now – would ever have attempted such a thing. But no matter. We had much daylight left and so little distance to go, the Bird could take his sweet time, and we hoped he would.

By that stage in the game we were starting to get surly owing to tight boots and those blasted swami belts. The water ran out. Jim smacked his thumb with the hammer. When the trail line snagged a pitch higher, instead of rappeling down to free it, I simply yanked as hard as I could, eventually pulling off a granite block the size of a Shetland pony. 'You imbecile!' Bridwell yelled. 'What if you'd cut the rope. Then what would we do?'

Fatigue was catching up, an open invitation for a mishap. We briefly discussed this – or rather, we listened to Bridwell expound on the point and I remain amazed at such times Jim would sound exactly like Franklin Delano Roosevelt. We regrouped. Bridwell hammered on.

We started relaxing a bit more at hanging belays, smoking cigarettes, and waving to all our friends who were parked in the meadow and honking horns, urging us to get the lead out. We loafed through another couple of pitches, but at Camp 6, "summit fever" took hold and we started driving for the top. By the time we gained the bolt ladder leading up the summit headwall, our waists were so trashed and our feet so sore we just wanted off.

Other routes are steeper, more exposed than The Nose, but no route has a more dramatic climax. The headwall is short (fifty feet) and once climbed, everything ends abruptly after a few friction steps. But since Harding's day, some madman had re-engineered the last belay so that it hangs at the very brink of the headwall, where all thirty-four pitches spill beneath your boots. Cars creep along the loop three-quarters of a mile below, broad forests appear as brushed green carpets, and for one immortal moment, you feel a giant in a world of ants.

From the start, with the exception of those brief smoke breaks, I stayed focused on moving fast. But when Jim scrambled to the top and yelled for me to hustle up, I couldn't move. I kicked back in my stirrups and looked around. I didn't know why. I had never lingered before, always pressing on with gritted teeth, surging, fighting both myself and the climb to gain the top. Suddenly I was free of all the incessant rushing. I just hung there and took it in, and for the first time in my climbing career I seemed to fully appreciate the fantastic nature of what I was doing.

The reverie lasted about a minute. Without knowing it, from the moment I'd first laced up climbing shoes I'd been chasing that experience, and found it only when I let myself linger for a beat. Yet even then I couldn't really recognize the tune. Finally, I stepped from the anchor and stumbled to the top.

On the summit there was no celebration. We didn't so much as shake hands. Topping out on El Capitan after the first one-day ascent should have been one of those few momentous occasions in our lives. But little registered but our throbbing feet. I only remember coiling ropes and slogging for the East Ledges descent route, everyone cussing at having not brought a pair of tennis shoes. We got down to the loop road just as darkness fell.

Drained by the nervous depression that always follows a wall, we stumbled around a bend and El Capitan burst into view, shimmering under a full moon. If there is anything whose magnitude can blow a person off his feet, it's that first ground-level view of a wall you've just climbed. The second we saw El Cap, we three stumbled out into the middle of the road and gaped up with open mouths. The Nose looked ten miles high. And how long it seemed we'd been up there, and how strange, as though we'd seen it in a movie, or in a dream, and had suddenly woken up, half remembering what we had dreamed.

Smiling at the great rock, Bridwell blew out a cloud of Camel smoke and said, 'Boys, we'll all do harder things. But a first like this can only be done once, and we'll never top it.' My feet suddenly felt fine, and the majesty of the cliff, and what it meant to us to have climbed it in one day, finally struck home.

Far left: Dean Potter on the Stoveleg Cracks during a speed ascent of The Nose of El Capitan

Left: Tim O'Neill on the King Swing, El Capitan

Below: O'Neill powers up the 5.11b climbing on the Pancake Flake of The Nose of El Capitan during a speed ascent

18 ENCHAÎNEMENTS AND RECORDS

How was it to continue? It is in the nature of sport, that with time, everything would have to be faster, higher and further. Time was even being reduced on the big walls of Yosemite. A day here, an hour there, minutes off. Every record was systematically broken and free climbers were steadily taking over in the speed race. The pure speed ascents were not (and are still not) solely free climbed but highly skilled free climbers hold a clear advantage as they are able to move quickly on otherwise time-consuming aid sections.

Soon one big wall in a day was not enough either. A dream had been floating round John Bachar's head for a while. It was to climb the two most significant routes in America in one day – linking up major climbing targets is what the French refer to as *enchaînements*. Bachar certainly felt he was capable of linking the thirty-four pitches of The Nose with the twenty-four pitches of the Regular Route of Half Dome. He just needed a partner who matched his own strength. That would be the only way he would achieve this feat. The rising Yosemite star in 1985 was the Canadian Peter Croft. As a gifted free climber Croft had already made a name for himself in the Valley. Croft climbed hard, safe and fast. Bachar had found his man.

The incredible length of the climb would require different methods of protection. Jumars and Friends had long been used on a regular basis but even with these assets it was still time-consuming to place a lot of protection. To be fast they had to 'run it out' and to make that work they had to have total reliance on each others skills.

They began on El Capitan at midnight, as Bachar described:

'It would take us about ten to fifteen minutes per pitch. You don't have to be frantic in your climbing, you just have to keep moving – we'd get to a belay and set it up in twenty seconds instead of two or three minutes. Little things like that are the key.'[5]

They topped in about ten hours, descended rapidly over the East Ledges, and made their way to the Regular Route on Half Dome arriving at one o'clock to begin their second big wall ascent of the day. To be faster they decided to climb all the middle grade free-climbing pitches simultaneously. They sprinted up the cracks and chimneys, rarely using anything more than a belay station for protection. It was all going smoothly, well, almost, until a thunderstorm took them by surprise just below the summit. Bachar was worried:

'It rained really hard and there was lightning everywhere. Our hair was sticking up from the lightning and the cracks were actually buzzing. We thought we were gonna get wasted, especially since all we had on were T-shirts and shorts.'[5]

Luckily the storm passed quickly and by six in the evening, they had reached the top.

After completing El Capitan and Half Dome in a day, Croft knew that he was capable of more. In 1986, his thoughts turned to the possibility of adding Salathé Wall to an ascent of The Nose in place of Half Dome's Regular Route. The pitches would increase from fifty-four to seventy. In addition, there was the comparatively greater difficulty of the Salathé, and the fact that it all had to be done in a day. Bachar was no longer available having by then withdrawn from Valley life so Croft looked for a new partner.

In 1990 he decided on Dave Schultz, an ambitious free climber. With their target chosen, they worked on perfecting their speed tactics. They would climb it in "blocks". One of the blocks was the thirteen pitches from Sickle Ledge to Boot Flake. They would 'simul-climb' this as the set-up of belay stations would take up too much time and changing leads would waste precious minutes. Croft had practised this style with Bachar several times on the easier sections of Half Dome. He and Schultz now regularly climbed 5.11 routes simultaneously. Because weight would slow down the speed, the climbing rack was reduced to an absolute minimum – just a handful of Friends and a few karabiners. Even on difficult pitches, there was often only one clipped belay station between the two climbers.

Schultz described the risks involved:

> 'We climbed pitches of 1500 feet without stopping. The dangerous part is that if the second would fall with the top guy sixty foot out or so, there was no way the top guy could hold the bottom guy. The leader would be pulled like a vacuum towards the last piece.'[5]

Trust in one's partner is absolutely essential, continuous and indispensable. It paid off in the end. Croft and Schultz broke several records at once. The six-hour ascent of The Nose, the ten-hour ascent of the Salathé and twenty-and-a-half hours for the two together, all three being substantial records in their own right.

The speed scene now began to grow steadily. Initially Bridwell, Bachar and Croft were not presented with any real competition, but as the numbers of speed climbers increased the competition intensified. Speed-climbing craze took hold in the

Valley. Records now only stand for a short time, each one just a little blip in climbing history.

In 1999, Hans Florine took part in a duel with his younger counterpart, Dean Potter. Their goal was to climb Half Dome and El Cap solo, in a day. Potter had dreamt of this combination for a while but when friends informed him of Florine's plans, he flew down from Colorado, hopped in a taxi, went straight up The Nose and was standing on top of Half Dome twenty-three hours later. Florine did not get wind of this and so set off the next morning on his own attempt. He raced up the Regular Route and then ran down into the Valley. There, he bumped into Steve Schneider who told him that Potter had successfully achieved the twenty-four-hour link up just the day before. Florine did not give up. Although no longer in the running for first place, he still had a chance of being the first to break the new record. And he did break it. Even though he had not been the first he felt he was the winner as he made the link-up in a faster time.

It is interesting to note that the whole story of "Speed" in the Valley centres almost wholly on the venerable old Nose. Whether for a solo or team ascent – in a link-up (enchaînement) or just for itself – the speed scene has not found a match for The Nose. The Nose will always remain an arena in which vanity is nurtured; the real highlight of any record in Yosemite.

True to Croft's character, he could not let The Nose record stand for very long. Croft had become a real expert on his favourite race track. He knew all the tricks, all the crux moves and all the cracks inside out, key factors when trying to set speed records. He made use of all of these advantages when he set the long-term record of four hours, twenty-two minutes

Dean Potter on the Stoveleg Cracks on The Nose, El Capitan

'Dean took the lead for the last block. Just six pitches to go. At every protection point, he would pull the rope up, fix it and carry on. I would then follow using jumars. As we both raced up the bolt ladder of the last pitch, I dropped one of my aiders and it disappeared into the void. Dean topped out and then ran around the next tree and carried on further in order to give me support on the last few metres of the bolt ladder. I could not even see him as I reached the tree and stopped the watch.'

Three hours, fifty-nine minutes, thirty-five seconds. The record which had stood for seven years was now broken and the young generation lay claim to The Nose. Hans Florine congratulated the two and made his own plans. It was less than two weeks before he hit back. On 28 October the record was broken again. The time he and Jim Herson finished in was three hours, fifty-seven minutes, twenty-seven seconds. But Potter and O'Neill were still in the Valley and on 2 November completed The Nose in three hours, twenty-four minutes, four seconds. It was only a matter of time before the route was done in less than three hours and in October 2002 Yuji Hirayama and Hans Florine did it in two hours, forty-eight minutes, twenty seconds.

with Hans Florine in 1993. In Harding's time it was the months which were counted, in Robbins's time it was the days and in Bridwell's time it was the hours. Now, even the minutes mattered.

This record became the longest standing of any to be set in the Valley. It was only natural, however, that it too would have to be broken at some point in the new century.

The showdown took place in October 2001 when Dean Potter and Tim O'Neill met up in the Valley. Water, food and T-shirts, anything which could slow them down were left behind. Ready, steady, go ... After seven pitches in twenty-six minutes, they changed the lead. Potter finished the first block and went on to lead the next ten-pitch sprint to Boot Flake, the second lead target. The first half of The Nose lay behind them after no more than ninety-six minutes.

*In May 2003 Alexander and Thomas Huber climbed Zodiac in two hours, thirty-one minutes, twenty seconds, which is currently the fastest time recorded on a major El Capitan route. Zodiac (seventeen pitches) is only half the length of The Nose and other classic routes in the central section, but is steeper and has harder climbing.

Balancing on a slack line is one of Yosemite's traditions

Above left: Dean Potter on Lost Arrow

Above top: Leo Houlding takes risks

Below left: Dean Potter on Rostrum with no protection whatsoever

Above: Old-timer Chongo Chuck

Right: Dean Potter on Lost Arrow half-way between Valley and heaven

Dean Potter

19 ENTRANCED BY THE FLIGHT OF A RAVEN

Entranced by the flight of a raven, I watch its shadow move effortlessly against golden, shimmering granite. I long to be that free, flying above the cluttered world of normalcy, where so many are half alive. I stare at Half Dome, watching the shadow from the setting sun race up its sheer face. Cool air floods the Valley floor and smells of evening call me to my bivvy site and sleep. Still, the image of the black bird soars throughout my dreams.

Morning comes, and I am sure. I grab my carefully readied equipment, and head towards the North-West Face on Half Dome. Clouds drift over the peaks, and in the forest I am misted with slight drops of rain. Emotions and wants rush in, but I concentrate on each breath and quiet my mind. My legs effortlessly take me up the smooth water-polished slabs, past wild flowers at the end of their bloom, to the base of the wall.

Fog overtakes the cliff as I walk below it, and the unstable weather frees me from the expectation of soloing the 2000ft wall. I near the route and see a team rappelling off, from about half-way up. I sit calmly watching them retreat and stare at the intricacies of the face, following the black water streaks to the top. The clouds are thinning. I become completely immersed in my senses … the smell of damp rock, the heat rising off my body, creating steam as it meets the chilled air, the hum of the wind as it hits the wall and, most powerfully, my instinct to climb.

I've thought about speed soloing the Regular for many years, yet as my hands reach out and touch the opening holds, no thought registers in my mind. I feel my fingers take every lock perfectly and I move without fear, because falling is not within my reality. Absolutely focused on my connection with the rock,

I barely notice the party of two rappelling twenty feet to my side. Their foreign questions float in the air, they disappear into the fog below me. I calm myself with a mantra from a favourite song, and repeat, 'I'm invisible, I'm invisible, I'm invisible …' I leave the ground behind.

I exit a shaded chimney, two-thirds of the way up the face. Any uncertainty I have is released with the sight of the sun pushing over the top and the clouds magically lifting. A raven call emerges in my throat and leaves my open mouth. Life pulses in my veins. Though I acknowledge the delicateness of my existence, I flow confidently through the insecure crux, the Zig Zags. The pads of my feet glueing to textured rock, my fingers securely clamping whatever they touch, I consciously drive out pressing anticipation of completion as I crawl across Thank God Ledge and scramble to the summit. Calmly spinning, I scan as far away as I can see. The last rays of the day's sun warm my back and my stare locks onto my own shadow. I follow the lines of my body on the stone in front of me, spreading my arms as wings, and bathe in the beauty of existence.

Editor's note: The photographs of Potter soloing this climb, and many others in this book, are not of the original ascent but are taken on a specially set up photo session to recreate the feel of the ascent but seen from the best possible viewpoint. True first-ascent or repeat ascent pictures (such as Tom Frost's Salathé and NA Wall shots) are usually obvious by their less than ideal positions and the more shambolic and strained look of the climbers.

Dean Potter soloing third pitch of the Zig Zags, the three marvellous crack pitches that form the climax of the Regular Route on Half Dome. These are either aided, semi-aided or climbed free at 5.12a, 5.10b and 5.12b

118

Left: Dean Potter on the final pitch (5.12b) of the Zig Zags. Soloists would normally climb the harder parts of this aiding from two or three slings from nuts or friends

Above and right: On the Thank God Ledge

Wolfgang Güllich making the first solo ascent of
Separate Reality (5.11d) in 1986

20 FREE SOLO

There are many opportunities to set greater challenges in climbing, even without pursuing first ascents. Take a stop-watch and you are speed climbing. Avoid pulling on technical aids and you are free climbing. Take nothing whatsoever in the form of gear and you are now "free soloing". This term is used to differentiate it from roped soloing that might involve aid or runners – though on smaller routes the term "soloing" still serves to describe the unprotected activity as self protection is rarely employed in such situations.

Free soloing in Yosemite commands a higher status than anywhere else in the world. So much has been written about it that one would imagine all climbers free solo. It is deceptive however. It has only ever been the pastime of a small élite. Even today, the number who consistently practise free soloing at a high standard can be counted on one hand. Climbing without any form of protection at all or any contingency plan for safety is too forbidding for it to ever become as popular as speed climbing for example. This is an activity for those with a cool and precise knowledge of their own ability.

The realities of free soloing are obvious. Proceed up your selected climb and take great care to retain control and concentration as the penalty for error is likely to be terminal. Generally if the holds are positive the situation should remain fully in the climber's control – the cruxes are usually associated with moves (friction, stemming etc) where there is no stopping hold, however small. Tom Patey, a well-known British soloist, once opined 'a soloer must be safe, otherwise he would be dead'.

When Henry Barber free soloed the Steck/Salathé on the Sentinel in 1973, it was not because he had long dreamt of such a feat. It was simply the spontaneous act of a talented climber who was comfortable with this grade of difficulty. Not able to find a partner, he

swiftly completed the route on his own, without any previous experience of the face. Even though he carried on to free solo Moby Dick Ahab (5.10b), in Yosemite he is not regarded as a "free soloist" because he only did it occasionally. However, his later on-sight solo ascent (in front of TV cameras) of The Strand (5.10c) on the Anglesey cliffs of Wales and other feats suggest that he fully merits the title.

In the history of climbing, real free solo climbers who operate at the highest standards are few. Their implicit mastery always commands the greatest of respect. From the beginning of the last century, and in Yosemite to this day, no other free soloist has been able to match Paul Preuss for his rigorousness but it is well to remember that Preuss died while soloing.

Then there was John Bachar.

> 'I started free soloing for a lot of reasons, one is freedom. It's such a great feeling to be unhindered by gear, just moving. I also realised that I could do a lot more climbing. It's not challenging as far as figuring out new moves, but it's challenging spiritually and mentally. Soloing to some people was a crazy, taboo type of thing. But it seemed logical to me – lizards and frogs crawl up El Cap without a rope, so why can't humans do that too?'[5]

He stuck to a daily soloing routine. With every season his free solo outings would become more extreme. When he free soloed New Dimensions (5.11a) and Butterballs (5.11c) Yosemite regulars just shook their heads in amazement. Bachar did have a close call in 1981 during an on-sight free solo of Moratorium (5.11b), a route unknown to him. A solo ascent done on sight is far harder than a climb previously done with a rope. The route's four beautifully choppy pitches harbour in them a demon crux move – the

Five years later there was another notable ascent
which Heinz Zak was there to record:

'200 metres above the Merced there is a fantastic
splitter crack through a six-metre horizontal roof.
Separate Reality, as it is known, was first climbed
by Ron Kauk and was not only one of the
toughest routes but was also representative of
the new climbing generation and its lifestyle. The
route is still seen as the epitome of free climbing.
Just as you come to the lip of the roof, the crux
move requires you flip your legs around to the
lip. On 11 October 1986, Wolfgang Güllich
climbed it free solo! His movements were precise
and smooth – the statement of a new
generation!'

As Heinz Zak's photos and the news of Güllich's
climbing feat circulated the climbing world, one of
Bachar's followers quietly rose to the surface. Peter
Croft set about climbing in the same style and with
just as much passion. Day after day, he achieved
incredible targets, all in a relaxed manner few could
emulate even when roped up. He free soloed routes as
tough as Fish Crack (5.12b) and would solo up to
thirty pitches in a day. His first milestone came in 1985
on the Regular (A1/5.7) on Rostrum. This nine-pitch
route had taken Harding and Denny days to complete
in 1962. Ron Kauk and John Yablonski first climbed it
free (5.11c) in 1977 and now Croft was free soloing
it. The quiet Croft seems to have a skill and steadiness
far beyond normality. His reputation as a top crack
climber was cemented with his on-sight roped leads
of Phoenix (5.13a) and Cosmic Debris (5.13b) but his
real masterpiece came in 1987 with his free solo
ascent of Astroman (5.11c) on Washington Column.
In Yosemite this was such an incredible feat that it
has still not been beaten and has only ever been
repeated once – thirteen years later by Dean Potter.

crack of a right-facing, open layback corner that gets
smaller and smaller until only fingertips width with, on
either side, expanses of smooth featureless granite with
no footholds and no handholds. Bachar began
to sweat. His feet were shaking and his climbing flow
had been broken. There was no going back. The choice
was quite simply to forge ahead or to fall. Bachar is still
alive today but his escape was narrow.

Peter Croft

21 Astroman —
A Comic Book Flight Manual

There are many reasons why people solo. Whether it is rock-climbing or long-distance sailing, motivations run the full gamut from patriotic fervour to semi-suicidal rage over some defunct relationship. For me, it stems from my childhood. No dark secrets there, just countless hours spent living in Superman comics and Tarzan movies. From there it only grew deeper but when I realised I would not be living with apes in Africa or flying faster than a speeding bullet I cast about for other ideas that might be a bit more manageable. When I finally discovered climbing I felt transformed, and then, years later when I first left the rope on the ground, it happened again.

After my first trip to Yosemite I was convinced of three things. The Valley was *the* place, free climbing was *the* game and Astroman was *the* route. Twelve hundred feet of perfect orange granite split by one of the most beautiful cracklines in the world. By the time I worked up the courage to try it (with a rope) it had assumed humungous proportions in my head. I didn't sleep a wink the night before and, once on it, was so nervous I practically shook my way to the top. At that time, the idea that anyone could solo it never entered my head.

Years went by, I climbed Astroman a few more times. At that time I had no thought of soloing Astroman. In fact you could really say it happened by accident. In 1987 I found myself enjoying the hot summer months of December and January at Mt. Arapiles, Australia. I was going for big mileage days down there, soloing all over the fantastic quartzite and when not doing that, running, increasing my mileage almost every day. My plan was to be in good shape so that when I got back to the Valley in May I could try some really big link-ups of a bunch of the old classics. But my big plans went bust when I blew a hamstring and couldn't run any more and so, with a

huge stockpile of pent up energy, I focused exclusively on climbing. When I returned to the Valley I was climbing more than ever and almost always by myself. It wasn't until then that Astroman filled my head.

I wanted to approach the perfect experience. A couple of years earlier when I first soloed the Rostrum I climbed it with a rope the day before to check it out and this had always bugged me. It had now been four or five years since my last ascent of Astroman and I decided that, although it couldn't be on sight, I would not make the same mistake again.

On that day I was very aware of the history of soloing in the Valley. John Bachar's ascents of New Dimensions and Nabisco Wall are landmarks there and so it made sense to start with those. Next I drove up to Curry Village and then, because it was very hot, walked out to the river to wait for Astroman to go into shade. It seemed to take forever. Finally it was time to begin and as I made my way up the talus to the start I was already in climbing mode, placing my feet with exaggerated care on the slidy slope. In my head it seemed very important that when I got to the base I should feel that I had already started.

The first 200ft went easily up to the Boulder Pitch. This, I knew, would be the crux for me: fingertip liebacking with specks for footholds. Perched in the launch position, if a foot blew it would be a *big* mistake. I climbed up and down two or three times and then went for it. I didn't so much stand on the tiny edges as meld my feet into them while I willed my fingers into the crack. It was all over in about a hundred heartbeats and I was released onto the upper wall.

The Endurance Corner was next and with hands plugged deep I jammed and then liebacked the awesome crack, pausing in a couple of spots to grin at the growing exposure. A few hundred feet of perfect hand cracks led to the dreaded Harding Slot. A little liebacking, a little jamming and then a fair bit of wiggling to get through. It felt almost easy and my psyche was soaring. Thoughts were sparking around in my head and I was climbing fast, hardly chalking up and then climbing faster. The next tricky bit is some funky barndoor moves above a small roof, but the finger jams felt so good that when the crack pinched off I just pasted my feet way up high and made a straightforward reach to some good holds. Fifty feet higher I stopped on a good ledge.

I was too jacked up, I realised, and was climbing too fast. If I continued like that, my margin for safety would be less and my appreciation of the whole adventure would be far shallower. So I sat on the

ledge, took off my shoes and gazed about. No one else was on the whole wall and the only sounds were the shrill cries of the swifts, tiny birds darting and diving about. Nobody knew where I was or what I was up to. And as I sat there idly kicking my bare feet in the air and looking over at Half Dome it all sank in. 'This is it,' I thought, 'this is what I came for.'

After a little while I started up again, climbing slower now and savouring every bit. The intricate fingercracks and faceholds of the Changing Corners which changes shape all the way up, the perfect cracked corners above going hand to fist and all of a sudden the last pitch, an easy corner to wide open face climbing. Twisty-turny side pulls and dinky pin scars getting easier to a final small overhang and the top.

Standing on the summit looking west towards El Cap and the beginning of a sunset I was super happy yet sort of sad. It was over. I looked from warm sunshine to dark shadows beneath me. Far below on the Valley floor was a different world that I was hesitant to re-enter. I waited a long time before I started down.

Later that summer I went back two or three more times, trying to recapture it all. I would start with Astroman, then head down the Valley and climb a bunch more, foolishly hoping that by simply adding to it I could duplicate the experience. The last time, I started with Astroman, then climbed the slightly smaller Rostrum and then drove down to the Cookie Cliff where I did all of my favourite routes. Fantastic climbs with great names: Crack-a-Go-Go, Red Zinger, Nabisco Wall and many more. But it didn't work. In a way, the more I added to it, the less it became. So I stopped trying and moved on.

Most of us dream of flying. Or at least we did when we were kids. A large part of it probably is about actually flying. But I'll bet it's also a bit of a metaphor for wanting to be, at least once, clearly better than who we are. To make that jump requires risk. Certainly I could have climbed Astroman with a partner and a rope. But by not being tied to the ground, for a brief moment, I was able to fly.

Croft leading Astroman's Endurance Corner (5.11c)

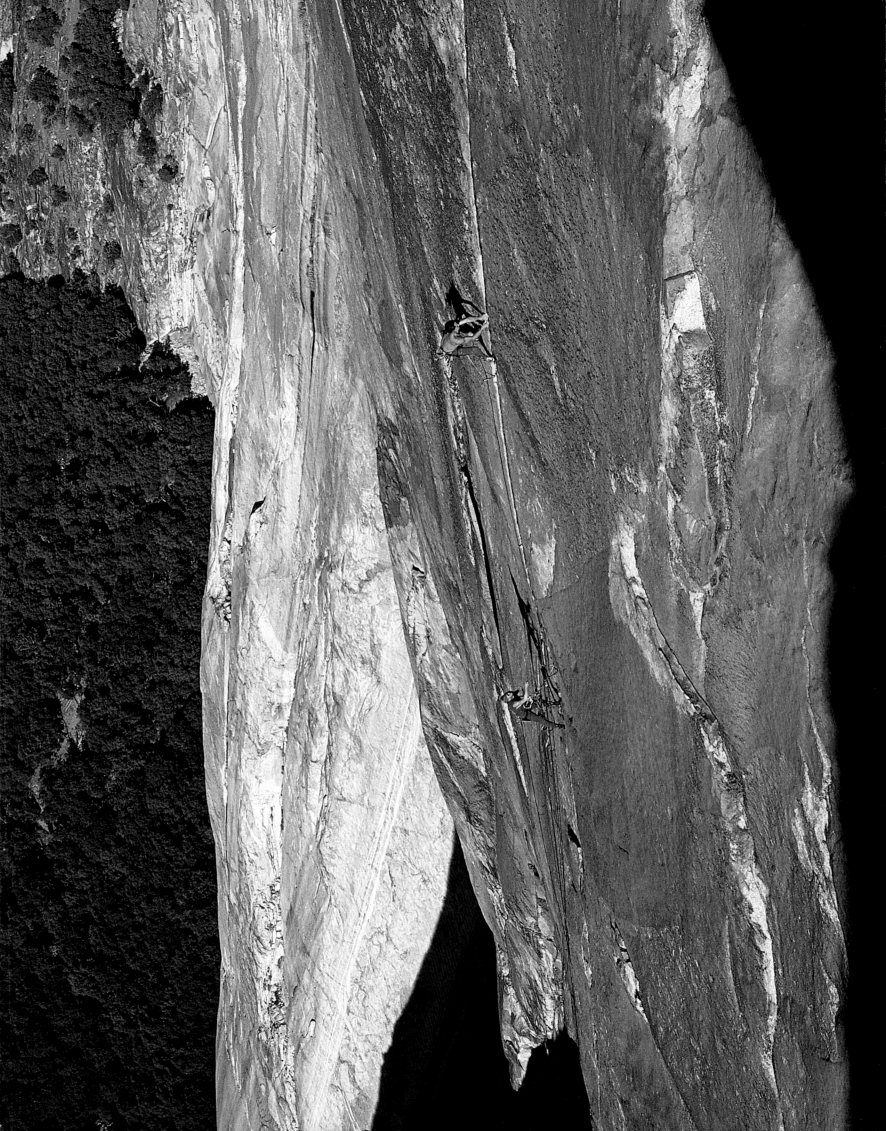

22 Freeing the Big Walls

The 1970s saw a free-climbing wave sweep across Yosemite. The action was not just limited to short hard routes, as the free ascent of Astroman demonstrated that bigger targets were also within reach. Despite this, the big walls were still the last frontier to be ventured upon by free climbers.

By 1976, Art Higbee and Jim Erickson from Colorado were making their way up the Regular Route on Half Dome. This was the ideal target for a first free attempt on a big wall, as large sections of the route have free climbing of middling difficulty anyway. Just a few bolt ladders and a section close to the summit remained as major obstacles. Unfortunately, it was not quite so easy for Higbee and Erickson to follow the path set by the first ascentionists. The section taken by the bolt ladder on the fourth pitch turned out to be unclimbable and so they were forced to work out a new three-pitch variation to the left. They even devised a way to bypass Robbins's Traverse. Sadly, on the penultimate pitch, they had to concede defeat and resort to aid. It was only later that Erickson cracked those illusive few metres – free climbing them while being top-roped from the summit Although not done in perfect style, this became the acknowledged first free ascent (5.12b) of a Yosemite big wall. The stylistically correct free ascent of the Regular Route finally took place in May 1979 when Leonard Coyne accompanied by Dennis Jackson and Doug Lorrimer freed the climb in a single three-day push.

At end of the 1970s Ray Jardine entered the big-wall-freeing arena. His first free ascent of the West Face of El Capitan (5.11b) with Bill Price gave him a taste for more and in 1981 he turned his attentions to The Nose. Many sections of The Nose were by then being routinely free climbed but there were still a number of stubborn aided passages to overcome that might require new variations. The major problems were the King Swing, the Great Roof and the steep cracks above Camp VI.

Jardine found a possible solution to the King Swing, whilst studying the face through a telescope from El Cap Meadows. He spotted what appeared to be a series of holds leading up to the left to join another crack system. If he could just bridge this twelve-metre gap, he would be in a position to overcome the first hurdle on The Nose.

But the traverse was simply too tough for Jardine. So he went for a solution for which most climbers judged him very severely. With the help of hammer and chisel, he created the Jardine Traverse, a series of artificial holds, which brought these metres of granite down to his level. Nevertheless, nobody has yet found another way and the chiselled Jardine Traverse still forms part of the free way up The Nose.

In an interview in 1995 Jardine explained his action:

> 'Was I committing a moral injustice or making a little bit of history? My vision was for a moderate route up the South Buttress of El Cap. I wanted to make it not of the highest standard but of the highest meaning. After I realized that enhancing face holds was not the way to go, I quit the project.'[9]

Although many of Jardine's visions were way ahead of his time, he appeared not to understand or accept that the essence of free climbing lay in adapting one's own personal skill to the rock and not the other way round. Instead of leaving a masterpiece behind on The Nose, what he did leave was the end of his climbing career. He eventually said goodbye to the world of climbing altogether.

Whilst heated debate still raged over Jardine's activities, others turned their attentions to freeing the big walls. A new pair of contenders were the East Coast climbers Mark Hudon and Max Jones who demonstrated their intent with a one-day free ascent of Half Dome's Regular Route. Moving their attentions to El Capitan, they set their sights on the Salathé Wall as it offered an almost uninterrupted sequence of chimneys and cracks and therefore presented a clear opportunity for a free climb. They actually came pretty close to pulling it off. Except for the Headwall and two further pitches half-way up they managed it all free, climbing several 5.12 pitches. Although they failed to achieve a fine free ascent they did show that free climbing was possible *even* on El Capitan.

A completely new type of approach was eventually used to make the impossible become possible. This was employed by Todd Skinner and Paul Piana in 1988. They avoided a one-push attempt in favour of a series of exploratory attempts, always cracking more of the moves. After twenty days they had deciphered the whole of the Salathé Wall up to the Headwall.

On their next visit, they abseiled from the summit in order to practise the moves on the Headwall. After a further eight days on the wall they were ready to tackle the Salathé in one go. Pitch after pitch, they made progress, with one of them leading free and the other jumaring. By the sixth day, they had reached the roof below the Headwall. Here, Skinner managed the first pitch straight off. The second one however, involved several falls. It seemed they were in danger of losing the battle. Their supplies were slowly dwindling and at this stage the climbers were physically exhausted. They finally decided they would rest for a day.

The next day, their eighth on the wall, Skinner also overcame the second 5.13a headwall pitch. But there

was still one more hard section to overcome: the last fifteen metres of very steep climbing. It was Piana's lead.

Having re-taped his trashed hands and fingers Piana fought his way up the last pitch making a series of dynamic and desperate moves to finally break through to easier ground.

With this hard section behind them, they had overcome all difficulties of the route. The rest should have been easy but the exit very nearly resulted in disaster. Having reached the top Piana used a huge granite block to set up the belay and while Skinner jumared Piana began pulling up the haulbag. As Skinner was just arriving at the rim, the block came loose and set off down into the void. It cut through two of their three ropes but they survived because the remaining rope had been clipped to an old piton next to the block.

Piana's leg was broken and Skinner had broken ribs. It was a painful and near tragic end to what had been a forty-two-day struggle for the first team-free-ascent of the Salathé Wall.

But the excitement over their extraordinary feat soon changed as doubts emerged. Bill Hatcher photographed parts of the ascent though he was absent when the critical leads were made. Nevertheless he is confident about their claims having been greatly impressed by their fine teamwork, ingenuity, determination and meticulous attention to detail. Despite this the doubts grew as the years went by, and one after another prominent climber attempted the Salathé and failed.

There is no real proof to support the doubts and apart from some grading errors their account is otherwise plausible so Skinner and Piana have to be credited for what was certainly a determined and very advanced

climb that narrowly missed ending in disaster. But because of the doubts an event that should have been an inspiration, turned into another dampener – the acclaim absent, the praise muted.* The discontent was so deep that it was another few years before the scene recovered and any new impetus was forthcoming.

Five years later, the real breakthrough happened and opened the doors for a new era – Freeing the Big Walls. Lynn Hill's friend John Long suggested that she would find The Nose rewarding as a free-climbing route. Long was certain that Lynn's small fingers would work as her secret weapon. In late August 1993, she teamed up with Simon Nadin, an outstanding British all-round climber who was used to doing bold routes using traditional protection. After two days on the wall, having used the Jardine Traverse during the approach, they bivouacked on a ledge just below their next big challenge, the Great Roof.

The Great Roof pitch begins with a corner similar to an open book. Smooth on both "pages" the cut stretches some thirty metres above in a straight line and then veers off to the right until it finally finishes in a huge roof, stretching a further eight metres off to the right. In order to free climb it one has to jam one's fingers into a very slender crack for a prolonged series of uncling moves. This is precisely where Long had envisaged Lynn's slender fingers would be her secret weapon. Her first attempt ended half-way up the roof. On her second attempt, her reserves began to wane at the start of the toughest section, but sheer willpower drove her on. One of her feet slipped off a hold but she caught herself this time and fought on until she reached a small ledge, bumping into a rather shocked looking Croatian climber. Just as surprised as Lynn Hill herself, he had just witnessed the first free ascent of the Great Roof.

But the climb was not yet over. There was still the pitch above Camp VI, the so-called Changing Corners. This part had not been free climbed before and was rumoured to require extremely reachy moves. Sure enough this three-metre section proved too difficult and Hill and Nadin had to abandon their dream to free climb The Nose – at least for the moment. But Lynn Hill was far from giving up …

*Editor's Note: On Salathé Wall the pitch that has stopped a number of determined free attempts is a steep corner just above the Ear. The final fifteen metres of this involves three sections of very hard climbing with a bridging (stemming) no-hands rest between each section where protection can be placed in pin scars and a thin crack. Though well protected, progress between these resting points is extremely difficult to accomplish with only pin scars for holds. Skinner (5 foot,10 inches) says that he used a technique of locking his fingers and udging his thigh up on the wall to be locked into a friction position by his arm supported in the piton scar, thereby giving him critical additional height to reach the next piton scar. Bill Hatcher confirms that he had practised this method earlier on old peg scars during a hard ascent on the Cookie Cliff. Huber considers this pitch, which he practised (with runner protection from above) during his initial Salathé Wall ascent but has never led, to be at least 5.13c/d and thus close to the top sport-climbing standards of the day.

Lynn Hill turning the end of the Great Roof (5.13c) of The Nose during a redpoint ascent

Lynn Hill

23 THE NOSE FREE

At beginning of September I returned to Yosemite with Brooke Sandahl, a talented and passionate climber with an understated manner, who turned out to be one of my greatest allies on this landmark ascent. We hiked nine miles to the top of El Capitan, rappelled down to the pitch above Camp VI and set to work on this enigmatic section of climbing. Brooke focused on trying his own face-climbing variation; I focused on climbing the original line. Climbing up this corner demanded an ingenuity of movement that I had rarely ever encountered.

We spent three days working on this pitch, and by the end I had pieced together a sequence of moves that went together like a crazy dance. It was a tango of smears with my feet, tenuous stems, back steps and cross steps, lay backs and arm bars and pinches and palming manoeuvres. Ironically, instead of being stopped by the "reachy" variation, I discovered that the original route turned out to be much better suited for a person of my body dimensions. I was able to climb this pitch with only one fall. Brooke was not successful on his variant, but seeing how close I was to success he was keen to join me in our effort to make a free ascent of the entire route from bottom to top.

When we returned to The Nose a few days later we were well stocked with food and water, and we both felt a sense of harmony in this magical place. When we arrived at the Great Roof, after one familiarizing try I then made a successful free ascent on my first attempt.

The morning of our final day, I woke up on the ledge at Camp V, and looked straight up the pitches of the giant final dihedral to the Changing Corners pitch that would make or break our attempt. I had just dreamt that I had free climbed this pitch and I felt excited about what was soon to unfold. The weather was cool and I felt relaxed.

I started up knowing I would have to link the complex set of moves together exactly the way I had imagined them over the past several days. I had worked out a strange manoeuvre involving a bizarre contortion that seemed like a disappearing act. Using a carefully coordinated sequence of opposite pressures between my feet, hands, elbows and hips against the shallow walls of the corner, I turned my body 180 degrees around.

'That looks like a contortion only Houdini could imagine doing,' Brooke yelled up as I spun around from my double arm-bar contortion. When I reached the belay I felt a tingle of disbelief run through me. Though we had several pitches to go, none were as hard as this one.

A dark wall of clouds was rolling in overhead leaving a few raindrops. 'Looks like a storm,' said Brooke, 'we'd better punch it all the way to the top today.' Nothing is more miserable than being caught in a storm on El Cap. It takes only minutes for the cliff to become a sheet of water and for hypothermia to set in. The last pitch before the summit was one of the most exciting pitches I've ever done. With nearly 3000 feet of exposure on an overhanging wall at the lip of a bulge, this was a spectacular way to conclude such a monumental climb.

Brooke and I bivouacked on the summit, curled around a campfire next to "Mr. Captain": a venerable old Juniper tree that was gnarled from centuries of lightning strikes and winter blizzards. The storm passed and the evening sky was bright with stars and a fulsome moon. We huddled around the fire relishing its warmth, laughing and reliving the most powerful moments of our climb. I felt a wave of emotion rush knowing that the combination of both our dreams and efforts had led us to this historic moment.

El Capitan
The Nose

5.12c

5.10a

5.10d

5.11d

Boot
Flake

5.10c

5.10d

5.11c

5.12a

5.10d

El Cap
Tower

5.9

5.8

5.13d

Changing
Corners

5.10c

5.10b

Stoveleg
Cracks

5.10d

5.10a

5.12d

5.12a

5.9

5.11a

Sickle Ledge

Pancake
Flake

5.11c

5.11b

5.10c

5.13c

5.11b

Great
Roof

5.10d

24 It Goes Boys!

Lynn Hill's free ascent of The Nose was not only a landmark in women's climbing but also shook the world of men's climbing. Her words of "It goes, boys!" were provocative but true. She hadn't needed a large team to spread out the burden of obstacles. She climbed every metre of it herself.

Once again, The Nose upstaged everything else happening in the Valley, but at the same time as The Nose redpoint was taking place, another important big wall free attempt was underway. On 4 September 1993, Todd Skinner's large team claimed the first team-free-ascent of the Direct North-West Face (5.13c/d).

Skinner and Paul Piana had begun the work, but after about three weeks Piana quit having become disillusioned by the difficulties and the time involved. Skinner enlisted others to help: Steve Schneider, Scott Franklin, Nancy Feagin, Steve Bechtel, Chris Oates and Galen Rowell who was returning to the climb he had first attempted with Ed Cooper in 1963.

Skinner and Piana had quickly discovered that the aided exit from the Crescent Corner could not be climbed free and that a very steep slab to the left would have to be overcome for pitches 3 and 4 (both having 5.13 difficulties). After rap-bolting these pitches (placing bolts about every three metres) and setting up a bolted stance between them in a very steep position, it was clear that they would need much practice to redpoint it. The climbers therefore concentrated on the rest of the route that had one more 5.13 pitch, three at 5.12 and seven at 5.11. Most of these were led by members of the team and periodically they attempted pitch 3, which had been named the Sleepwalker because of its very marginal and delicate climbing. After nearly two months Skinner, belayed by Franklin, led this critical 5.13c/d pitch and on the sixty-third day Skinner, Bechtel and

Oates freed the remaining upper pitches and topped out on the summit of Half Dome.

This ascent would have been an important chapter in history had it not become the subject of controversy. Scott Franklin questioned the redpoint claim. Franklin was very qualified to comment being a leading sport climber and the first American to climb to 5.14.

> 'The story is I was belaying Todd when he *almost* redpointed the crux pitch. I say almost because instead of doing the last hard moves and standing up into a marginal no-hands stance he just grabbed a five-foot sling that he had hanging down from the anchor … if the sling hadn't been there, he would have fallen – hence it was not freed! The reasons I left the team were: in Todd's mind his ascent of that pitch was "good enough" and as long as all the individual pitches get freed by any member of the team, it is a free ascent. I completely disagree with both points and therefore left the team.'*

The code of free climbing is that if a sling is held to prevent a fall or to gain height, the pitch cannot be counted as having been climbed free.

When consulted, Skinner (supported by Steve Bechtel) strongly refuted this account stating that the sling on the stance was of normal length, not five feet, and he did grab it to clip in but only after the climbing had ended. Soon after this Franklin and Schneider left the project because of a financial disagreement.

The truth in this matter thus remains clouded, but the face was climbed in a team free ascent (or near ascent depending on whose account is correct) and certainly included some exceedingly hard climbing led, variously, by members of Skinner's disparate team – an early example of a "hotchpotch" style that was to become increasingly common on big wall free bids.

Far right: Wonderfully positioned moves on Bobby's Bunny Slopes (5.12c), El Corazón, El Capitan – a photo made more logical if turned sideways

Right: El Capitan from Taft Point

When I arrived in Yosemite in 1995, the debate over Skinner's free ascents was still raging. Despite all this, I still had my dream: the first redpoint ascent of the Salathé Wall (5.13b). I knew that this would not be easy as I was not the first one after Skinner and Piana to attempt to free climb the route. All those who had tried were forced to turn back half-way up the wall by the long shallow corner above the Ear. The whole story surrounding the Salathé seemed rather a deterrent but I would not be put off. I had at least to try. After weeks of training I got used to climbing on granite and its cracks. I felt I had a chance of redpointing the thirty-six pitches in a single push. Nevertheless, I did not always stick to the exact Skinner/Piana line of 1988. I chose the path of least resistance and avoided the section which had already shattered many dreams. There is no doubt that today the Salathé Wall is the absolute classic amongst the big free-climbing routes in Yosemite.

*E Mail to the author.

Editor's note: On Skinner's one lead of the Sleepwalker pitch, Franklin belayed, Bechtel and Oates watched from about forty-five metres to the side and Rod Fox filmed from a position close to the belay/abseil position at the top of the pitch. Bechtel's eye-witness account and that of Franklin do not tally. Franklin stayed with the party for two more days leading sections above Sleepwalker, and is also seen on the film congratulating Skinner. Skinner claims that this implies that Franklin was not critical at that point, though Franklin says he was naturally happy for Skinner on reaching his new high point on such a hard pitch, coming close to success after so much effort (falls, failures etc), but this did not mean it was a *redpoint*. Skinner wished to wait before the final push to allow Rowell to rejoin the team to take photographs for *Life* magazine. It was at this point that financial disagreements prompted Franklin and Schneider to leave the team. Asked why Franklin's name (and Schneider's) was left out of his *AAJ* account of the climb, Skinner admits that this was a mistake that he regrets. Skinner notes Fox's video clips show both the redpoint ascent and Franklin congratulating him in the aftermath, but thus far nobody other than Skinner and Fox has seen this. On such a complicated and drawn out saga, it is possible that memories of the precise events may soon become unreliable. Paul Piana's book (*Big Walls*, Sierra Club Books 1997) gives more detail of the financial disagreements but does not refer to any ethical dispute. The financial disputes that hinged around the media coverage that was planned in advance (shades of Harding) add a further aspect for consideration.

LAWBREAKERS

In 1994, Scott Cosgrove, Greg Epperson and Kurt Smith attempted a free ascent of Muir Wall. Their free bid failed just short of the top where they had to aid a short stretch of only a few metres giving them a climb graded A0/5.13b. Instead of a welcoming committee to greet them on top, they were faced with two park rangers. In order to set out new variations to the original route and replace old bolts, they had used a power drill. According to the National Park Statute, this is strictly forbidden in a protected wilderness area. The rangers immediately confiscated their equipment and all their photos and for their "crime", they ended up in court and each was fined $187.

25 REDPOINTING THE SALATHÉ

The Headwall on the Salathé is where I had dreamt of being ever since I first saw a picture of it. It is now May 1995, and although the dream finally comes true I am not that excited about being here. Gottfried Wallner and I have spent a wet and uncomfortable night in our bivouac. At daybreak, chilled to the bone, we struggle our way up the exposed face of the Headwall and the last few pitches of the Salathé Wall. Exhausted, we finally reach the summit plateau around noon to warming sunlight and an end to the toil. The reality of this big wall ascent had little to do with the dream I had nurtured in my head for years.

Nevertheless spending the last few days on the wall was still a valuable experience. I have a dream. It is the redpoint ascent of the Salathé, and I have just taken a step towards this. I have not been able to free climb all the pitches in the last couple of days but what I have learnt was that every move on the Salathé is possible to free climb. My dream is actually feasible. I found new variations to those parts of the Skinner/Piana 1988 route, which had presented insurmountable barriers to anyone attempting to follow in their steps. For example I had found a way of outflanking the long narrow crack above the Ear that had forced every subsequent attempt into failure. Studying the face in advance from the Meadows, I had noticed a wide crack about six metres to the left. A thin undercling flake makes possible the exposed traverse to gain the terrible fifty-metre offwidth. The Offwidth Monster is one of the worst of its sort. It is too narrow to disappear into and too wide to jam with arms or legs, only fierce off-width technique works. The moves are abnormally strenuous, irritating and time-consuming. It's a horror show: centimetre by centimetre you battle your way upwards, heading for release and redemption.

But with this fiendish Offwidth Monster I have bypassed the first crux point, which has stopped so many attempts. The path is clear!

Sunny California! It rains, it snows and I wait a whole week down in Yosemite Valley before the weather gods finally seem to see things my way. The weather report predicts rather changeable weather for the coming days but the general forecast is good. I am ready. I set off alone over the East Ledges to the summit of El Capitan. I have hardly reached the bivouac site under a little rock roof on the summit plateau when I get caught in yet another downpour.

I wait for two days in my sparse "hotel room", a tiny bivi hole, until the fine weather that has been forecast finally provides me with some relief. The next two days I spend hanging on jumars studying the moves on the Headwall. According to Todd Skinner's reports it went free in three pitches, two of 5.13a and one of 5.13b. However Skinner's stance, the same as that used on the first ascent, now sprouts new bolts. Bolts or no bolts it is still a hanging belay, which should not be used for a redpoint ascent where pitches should ideally be broken at full ropelength or where there is a no-hands rest. Adding this stance will make things far easier so these two shorter pitches should be run together.

The Headwall is a wall within a wall, and the crux of the Salathé. A V-shaped crack forms the start. It starts with climbing on the tiniest crimps up rounded edges until you can change over to the main crack. This splits the Headwall for seventy metres without rest or respite. It is climbed with flared handjams and towards the end a thin finger crack leading to a no-hands rest stance. The final shorter pitch above has an exquisite crack and ends with tricky 5.13b face climbing on a diminishing seam, all done while hanging 800m above the El Cap Meadows. But by then you have long got used to the dizzying abyss sucking at your heels.

I am back on the Valley floor again waiting for fine weather for a week. Finally, I go back up to El Capitan.

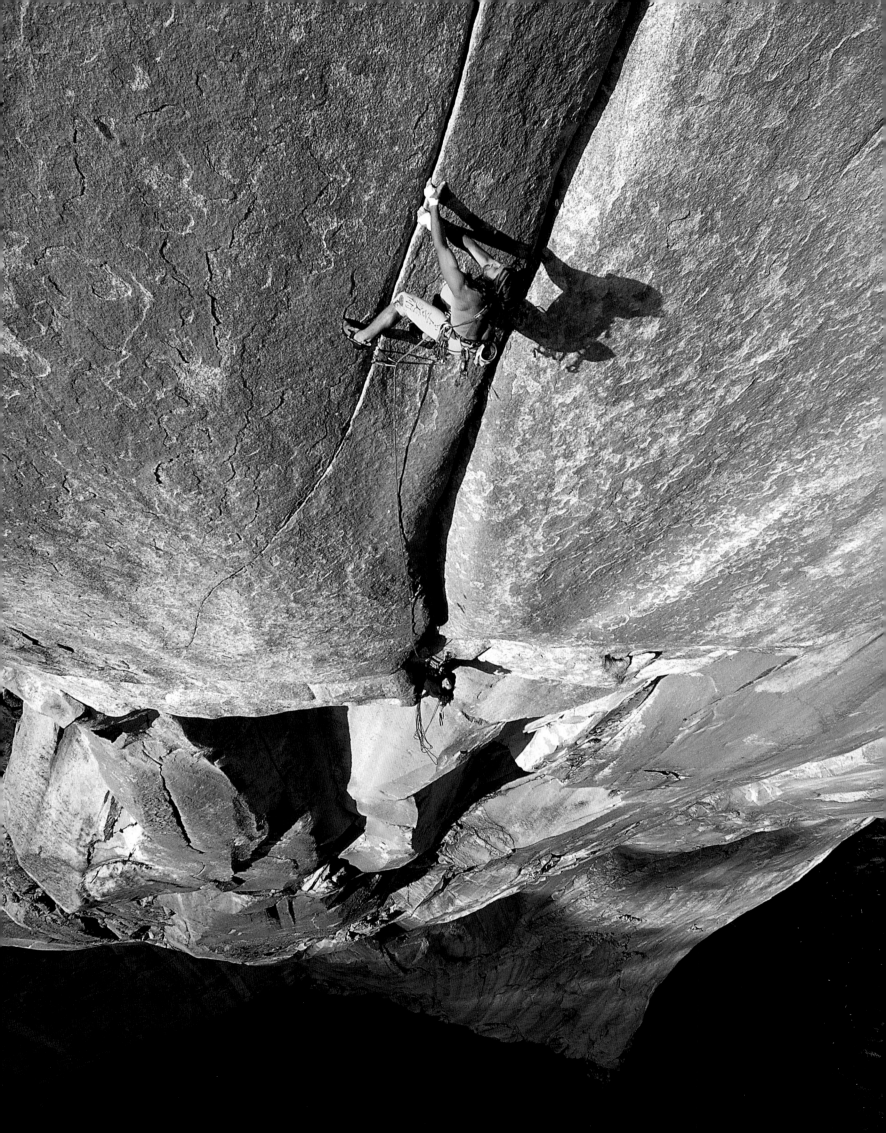

Only granite could be so perfect – the Picture Book Dihedral (5.12d) high on the Salathé Wall, El Capitan

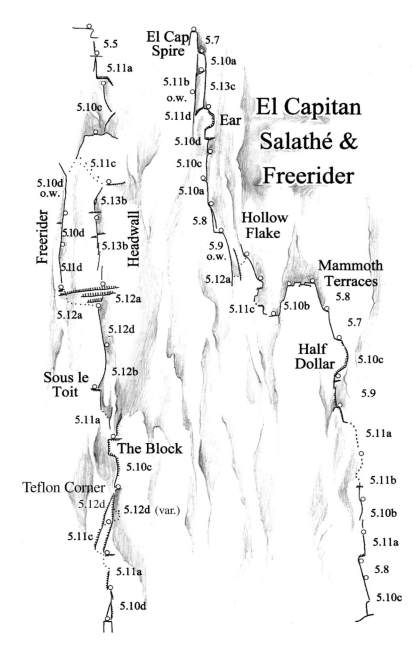

El Capitan Salathé & Freerider

Like a gymnast working on his routine, I work the moves once again until, two days later, Mark Chapman pays me a visit and offers to belay while I try to lead these crux pitches.

We abseil down Salathé's last five pitches to the start of the Headwall. I am nervous, damned nervous. Even so, as I begin the first pitch I am totally focussed. My field of vision narrows so I can only see the next jam. Slowly but steadily I make my way up this perfect cut with sometimes flared but never nasty handjams along this endless splitter – all in the middle of nowhere, the overhanging desert of this wildly exposed place. Finally, three metres from the belay I place my last Friend. Strength ebbing fast I pull on the rope. Nothing, no movement, the rope drag prevents me from clipping in. The last Friend is ten metres below and the next few metres will be the hardest. There is only one way to go … to move up and on – despite the risk of a big fall. Later I have no real idea how I managed it.

'Hey you guy, that runout was crazy!' Mark congratulates me, shaking his head. On the top, two hours later, we celebrate with Budweiser and chips the first redpoint ascent of possibly the best pitch in the world – for the best granite climbing … nothing comes close to El Capitan.

Now I am ready for the final continuous redpoint ascent of the whole route. In 1988, in the conventional style of the period, Skinner and Piana divided the route between them: each leading half of it while the other jumared. Things have moved on and now it is time for one person to lead the whole thing free.

Again I am back at the base of El Capitan this time with Heinz Zak. Two attempts have to be aborted because of bad weather, on the second the rain begins at the Heart Ledges so we fix our ropes and rappel to

the ground. Next morning, the weather finally seems more stable so we jumar to the Heart Ledges and resume the climb. Soon we are at the notorious Hollow Flake, the thirty-metre chimney with no means of protection. Here we catch up a slower party, who had been grappling with the pitch for some time. Unfortunately, as we overtake, there is a certain level of chaos costing both parties time and energy.

At 6 p.m. I arrive at El Cap Spire, pumped and completely spent but happy that the Monster Offwidth is finally behind me. It is getting late and in the gathering gloom, after climbing further taxing pitches, Heinz and I reach our planned bivouac site on the Block. I know that I have completed a first important step to a successful ascent.

The next day comes. There are only ten pitches above us, so we have lots of time. I have a really long lie-in and it is midday by the time I set off, somewhat stiffly, on the first pitch to the Sous Le Toit Ledge. Although not too hard it nevertheless demands a great deal from me. It takes a while before I feel, with relief, the fresh blood rinsing the trash of the previous day from my forearms. At the start of the Headwall, I am tremendously nervous and after only a few metres I take a fall. Annoyed with myself, I have to force myself to calm down, otherwise I will never manage it. Slowly, I become more relaxed, the tension evaporates and I start up the pitch again. Everything is reduced down to this one crack, in which my hands are now jammed. The crack has become a microcosm in the unending, featureless wilderness of its granite walls. Again, I have problems clipping the rope into the last piece of protection and yet again, on my last reserves of strength, I carry on without it for the last few metres. And I make it … I scream my joy to the world, drunk on adrenaline. After this critical pitch the final short 5.13b face climbing pitch presents no problem and after the final pitches we top out onto the summit plateau of El Capitan, I stare down into the void below, yet I see nothing. Only the inner film of memory is playing, a film of my dance up a thousand metres of granite.

Alex Huber (belayed by Linda Carillo) leading the final section of the big (5.13b) Headwall pitch of Salathé Wall. Note the overlap between leader and belayer that marks the position of the conventional hanging stance, and the distance of the last runner below the climber

The last tough move of the route (5.13b) … on the second pitch of the Headwall (a picture that gives an exaggerated impression of the angle which is about ten degrees over the vertical)

26 Big Walls Climbed Free and Fast

The redpoint ascents of The Nose and Salathé Wall meant the spell had been lifted. Free the big walls is today the most important aspect of what is going on in the Valley. From now not one year would go by without at least one of the greater big walls being freed.

As one would expect, the climbers worked on new styles of ascents. "Free Speed", consistent free climbing against the clock, is one of the recent challenges in the Valley. It has not had the greatest following since the requirements of free climbing go against those of speed. A difficult climbing move demands smooth motion, precise footwork and exact coordination. Rushing when on a technically difficult section of a wall could spell disaster. Forearms need a rest after hard moves otherwise you cannot carry on. "Free Speed" is thus a highly tactical game with two opposing factors. Number one, you must be able to redpoint the pitch but at a sensible pace. Only then will you be able to summon up enough energy to pull through the last few free moves on a big wall. "Free Speed" is not some mad race against time. The speed comes from the continual flow of precise, high level moves.

In 1994, Lynn Hill was the first to throw down the gauntlet against time. One year after completing the first redpoint ascent of The Nose, she went on to smash her own record. After the most thorough preparations, coherent training and precise tactical planning, she set off at 10 p.m. on 19 September 1994 with Steve Sutton as her belayer and redpointed all pitches in twenty-three hours. The world looked on in amazement. Today climbers hold that feat in the highest regard. Lynn Hill set the standard by which all free climbers would measure themselves on big walls. Her record of twenty-three hours, which still stands today, may in future, turn out to be the toughest of all speed records to break. In 1996, my brother Thomas tried to redpoint the Salathé Wall in one day. He had set his sights high and repeatedly fell short:

> 'I wanted too much. I wanted it all and for that I had to pay. It was only just before flying home that I could then just manage a two-day free ascent on which I failed to redpoint two pitches, only being able to overcome them by yo-yoing.'

One year later, it was Yuji Hirayama's dream to on-sight the Salathé. The prospect of transferring the idea of on-sight ascents from the realm of sport climbing to that of big walls, may not seem such a huge step at first. Apart from Hirayama however, not one person at that time thought it would be possible. His objective was just as visionary as Lynn Hill's one-day redpoint ascent of The Nose. As one of the best competition climbers, on-sight-climbers and one of the best all-round climbers in the world, Hirayama had what was required to make his dream come true. With his training in Yosemite including the on-sight ascent of the Love Supreme (5.13a) in the Tuolumne Meadows, he was well on his way. And once he got started (belayed by Hans Florine and Hidetaka Suzuki), there was no stopping him. The first section of the Salathé, was not a problem. When he reached the middle section and Skinner's Teflon Corner, the 5.12d pitch just below the Block, he had his first fall. Hirayama would not be put off. He readjusted the rope and carried on up the Huber variation on the right (also 5.12d) – on-sighting it! After a night spent in a bivouac on the Block, the journey continued up towards the Headwall. This is where the on-sight dreams finally vanished. Hirayama fell on both pitches, but redpointed them both on his second attempt. Hirayama and his team topped out just thirty-eight hours after leaving the Valley floor. Even though he did not fully realise his dream, Hirayama's ascent was an important signal for the future.

Peter Janschek in the Monster Offwidth (5.11b) variation pitch above the Ear on the Salathé Wall

Alexander and Thomas Huber on the third pitch (5.10d) of the Free Rider variation to the Salathé Headwall, El Capitan

27 AN EASIER SALATHÉ VARIATION: FREE RIDER

By 1995, I too was itching to do El Capitan in one day. I had found an alternative to the Salathé's difficult Headwall and had already soloed it. With that in place, I now knew that all the toughest parts of the Salathé were simple to bypass. This new alternative, Free Rider (5.12d), was therefore my best option for a one-day free ascent.

On my next trip to Yosemite in 1998, my brother and I were now fully prepared. Gear was pared down to an absolute minimum with one litre of water each, two energy bars and a bag bursting with chalk. It was mid-October and the daylight hours would not be enough, so we set off in the middle of the night. At 3 a.m. we stood at the base of the wall, hyped up and ready for Free Speed.

For the last time that day we fill up our bodies with water. We both stand roped up with our climbing shoes on, facing the black mass of granite. My hands sink into the chalk and using my head torch I lift off the ground at 3:31 a.m. We both know the Salathé very well. In the dark, we know where the holds are and we know in which direction we are heading. By sunrise, we already have the first eleven pitches, the Free Blast, behind us. The next determining obstacle will be the Monster Offwidth. It takes us one hour for that one pitch. After such physical torture, we stand astride the El Cap Spire and feel in need of a breather. It is eleven o'clock. We have eight hours of daylight left and fourteen pitches to go. Not long for such difficult climbing and we will be pushed, but we still need a twenty-minute break right now.

It is just before four o'clock when we move away from the Salathé. Thomas starts traversing to the left below the Headwall Roof. After five metres, just before the arête, the horizontal seam seems to vanish. But just around the arête there are the necessary holds to continue. Thomas gropes for the invisible holds, and soon disappears out of my sight. When I rejoin him we both feel pretty spent and have long since eaten our second energy bar. But now we follow perfect cracks, which split the otherwise featureless, golden granite. These are just as exposed and beautiful as the ones just around the corner on Salathé's Headwall, but they are less flared and therefore much easier to jam.

We rejoin the Salathé at the end of the Headwall. All tough spots are now behind us. Thomas follows up behind me. There are now two pitches left and less than one hour of daylight left. We have long since given up climbing purely for the sense of success. We now push on because we have no other option. We have no bivi gear and with the end in sight all we want is to be on top.

As the light begins to fade, I top-out and run a sling round a tree to belay Thomas up the last stretch. He reaches me at 18:56 with the last hues of light. Free Rider is completed in fifteen hours and twenty-five minutes. Even after such a long day, we cannot help but dance around the tree in celebration.

We sit down after one minute. Leaning against the trunk of the tree, we feel the calm after the storm return to our bodies and souls. We sit silently next to each other, too tired to talk. But we are still awake for a while and sit dreaming with our eyes open.

Page 152: Alexander Huber in the Black Dihedral (5.12c), El Niño, El Capitan, two pitches below the critical exit from the Black Cave

Page 153: Thomas Huber in the bottomless chimney of the Dolphin (5.12b) on El Niño – the pitch that provides an escape from the Cyclops Eye

*Thomas and Alexander on the summit
of El Capitan (left) and on the Royal Arch
(5.13b) El Niño, El Capitan*

Thomas Huber

28 El Niño — Freeing North America Wall

1998. The West Face, Salathé Wall, The Nose and the East Buttress, virtually all of the faces on El Capitan were opened up to free climbing it seemed. But not quite all. The huge South-East Face had still not been freed. The largely overhanging right flank of this face is covered in a tightly knit network of mostly extremely difficult aid routes. In 1964 the way up proved to be North America Wall, long hailed as the toughest big wall route in the world. An aid-climbing milestone in its day, now it promised to become a free-climbing milestone because it clearly offered the most climbable features on the whole of the South-East Face.

We sat in the Meadows and stared up at the vertical granite of El Cap, just as we had done so often before. Alexander zoomed in with the telescope and we compared our tentative plans with the reality of visible details which now faced us. Conrad Anker had given us some vital tips. When we asked him about North America Wall, he pulled out his secret topo of a possible free line on the right side of El Capitan. It was a line he had only just found last week with some friends. The idea is certainly bold but also brilliant. Even with our telescope and Conrad's drawing, we still cannot get the answers to all our questions. Is there really a free-climbable line between the first hold on the first pitch and the last hold on the last pitch?

Not wishing to waste time we drag our heavy packs to the foot of the wall. It is always an exciting moment to touch El Cap after a prolonged separation. I lean my head right back and follow the line of all my dreams and wish myself to a point over 900m above me. Right now it seems impossible but it is exactly the fact that it is unattainable which drives us on and dares us to risk this adventure. We see the best place for us to start at the Footstool, a small pointed buttress at the start of New Jersey Turnpike. We spend all of half a day on that route, only to find that we had come to a dead end. Conrad's advice is to overcome this part by passing it on the left. It looks like a good alternative! From the Footstool I can see a diorite vein, the Black Dike, cut through the otherwise featureless golden granite. Conrad had already climbed this pitch and placed some bolts.

We are back the next morning and find the easiest way through the Black Dike. The next section linking Black Dike and the Galapagos nearly ended our attempt because of a smooth patch between the belay and easier climbing on some chickenheads. A tiny flake, the only feature, breaks under the force of my fingers. For a moment we appear to have found another dead end until I notice that the remaining scar has left a two-millimetre-wide edge – just enough to make progress. The smallest detail has saved a 900m total package!

The Galapagos, the pitch that will bring us back to New Jersey Turnpike, will be the toughest pitch yet. Conrad's variation cost us a great deal of energy but it was worth it. The first stage has been conquered. We plan to spend the next five days on the wall finding a free line up the middle section of North America Wall. It will be the most exciting part of our mission with the most potentially difficult sections: the pendulum traverse and the huge roof of the Black Cave.

The way up to the bivouac site on the Big Sur gives us hardly any problems. By evening, we are settled with all our gear on the long metre-wide ledge. We are now on the west coast of the dark diorite patch that gives the shape of the North American continent – and so far still on solid ground …

By first light the next morning, we can see the
sparkling granite of the Pacific and our next obstacles,
the two pendulum traverses which should get us to
the Black Dihedral. On the former we manage to work
a free route. On the latter, however, our hopes are
dashed. Freeing the Right Side poses a problem. There
is no link. With the continuation just out of reach, we
search in vain but the path above is blocked. It feels
as though this passage is also the crux point of our
motivation. The art is in making the best of the
situation and often the route is more interesting when
an intricate way forward is found.

We discover a no-hands rest, eight metres below us.
From there, a shallow granite arch we named Royal
Arch, stretches to the left to the start of the Black
Dihedral. It looks difficult but if there is going to be
a solution to our dilemma, then this had to be it.

We still feel defeated though, defeated by a few
metres of blank granite and we have to put weight
on one of the pegs in order to abseil down those
eight metres. By the evening, the hiss of a beer can
opening and a huge slurp refreshes our thoughts
and prompts even wilder ones.

Alexander developed a theory on how to avoid
putting weight on one of the pegs. The solution to
the pending problem is a brand new concept plucked
from Alexander's collection of ideas. Instead of using
the peg to abseil from, we could use each other as
living belay stations. Alexander secures himself to the
station with a slack rope of about one metre and
holds the weight of my abseil to the no-hands rest
by sheer muscular strength. This little game acts as
an unconventional solution to a free-climbing
problem. We do not know whether others will accept
this 'manpowered rappel' as a valid solution, but we
are happy with it.

Alexander Huber emerging onto the lip of the Black Cave, perhaps the most dramatic section (5.13b) of El Niño

The aim is to get closer to the Black Cave and, so we believe, the last real obstacle in the way of the summit. Alexander begins to unravel the mystery. Right in the middle of the roof, he finds somewhere to rest and manages to stand without the use of his hands in a wild position.

The last six metres to the normal belay point look difficult and protection is pretty poor. There is a two-centimetre sawn-off angle peg left in a pinscar on the lip of the overhang. This dubious bit of pseudo-protection is the last we have at our disposal to protect the cross-over above this wild abyss. There are some who might be tempted to place a bolt to protect the climbing at this point. This would be totally unacceptable particularly on the most spectacular part of North America Wall. Not only would it attack Yosemite traditions but it would also be an offence to the legacy of the first ascentionists.

So this section has to be taken very seriously. Alexander makes several attempts at the cross-over and every time ends up climbing back to sit by our questionable protection. He has one more try and this time he cracks it (5.13b). There is no turning back now, for him. He swings his feet up onto the ledge and snatches the next hold with supreme control. He is now three metres past the sawn-off angle and only has another metre to go to the belay. He disappears above the edge of the roof. All I can do is wait and see. Wait to see him come flying through the air in a big arch or wait for his cry of joy as he reaches the anchors.

He screams. Luckily it is with joy. That son of a bitch has nerves of steel. Thirty-four years after Chuck Pratt had fought his way over that roof, Alexander had turned this spectacular stretch into free-climbing art.

We spend the next three days trying to find the easiest way through the upper part of the wall. We then sit on the top of our route, completely worn out, sweaty and caked in dirt. It has taken us a full two weeks to solve our puzzle. A lot of the time was spent following the existing route but due to hairline cracks, which were impossible to free climb, we were often forced to put up variations to the original route. The result is a mix of Continental Drift, New Jersey Turnpike, North America Wall, Sea of Dreams and numerous new variations. The combination of these has its own identity and a new route is formed. It is an indicator of change to the aid climbing on El Capitan: a fresh breeze is blowing, bringing a change of climate. Whilst the El Niño tides and winds have added climatic turbulence on the American continent, it is finger strength, muscles and chalk which are now starting to rule the roost on the South-East Face of El Capitan.

The first ascent is over and our curiosity abated. But the project is not yet finished. Only when we have both free climbed and redpointed El Niño, will we feel that we have reached the finish line. After two days of rest with drawn out breakfasts in the cafeteria and swimming in the Merced, our batteries are fully charged again. We are ready. So off we go. We both knock off the Black Dike and the Missing Link in one go but the Galapagos turns into a stumbling block. Alexander had already led the pitch redpoint. As I followed up, I swapped feet and lost my grip on a friction hold. I cannot let that happen again! After a short break at the belay, I look up at the Galapagos again and have the same electrifying feeling as when you are about to take the lead. It is the responsibility towards one's partner that you also feel when following. This time the foot swap works and it is not long before the first crux position is behind us. On the second day, we climb without any hiccups all

Pages 160 and 161: Alexander Huber on the Coffee Corner (5.13a) and the following Roof Traverse (5.13b), two of the key pitches of El Corazón, El Capitan

the way to the top of the Black Dihedral, hook up our ropes and abseil down to our camping spot on Big Sur.

On the morning of the third day, we climb the Black Cave straight off and the rest is just going through the paces. We are so absorbed in our climb that we do not notice the dark clouds brewing in the distance. With one hundred metres to go and all difficult stretches behind us, the rain starts to fall lightly. We speed up and climb at full speed. If we get caught in the storm here, there is no chance that we will manage to climb the exit face and will have to spend another night on the rock. We climb fast, as fast as we feel is just safe, to the very limit. We are lucky. A short while later we have topped out and stand on the summit. We slam our hands in a high-five to celebrate our victory. One thousand metres of climbing now lie beneath us, our hands are shredded and it starts to pour with rain.

Alexander Huber, belayed by Max Reichel, at the end
of the Roof Traverse (5.13b) – on El Corazón,
El Capitan

29 ADRENALINE – WHAT THE FUTURE HOLDS?

I lie in the dark of night with an overhanging cliff above my head, awake, in my sleeping bag. The moon must have risen over Half Dome in the east. Max Reichel and I are half-way up El Capitan and in the shadow of The Nose. The Yosemite Valley is lit up by the white light of the moon. El Corazón (5.13b) will be my fifth free-climbing route up El Capitan. Doing a big wall is nothing new for me these days, but I still get nervous at the start of every free ascent. It is the uncertainties and the lack of guaranteed success which make it hard yet so fulfilling for me. It is the adrenaline that stops me from sleeping that I cannot live without.

More and more climbers will want to free climb El Capitan in the future, as free climbing the big walls is the ultimate challenge in the Valley today. The trend only began quietly but the last few years have seen a huge increase in free ascents of big walls. I still clearly remember the autumn of 1998. Thomas and I had just climbed El Niño and were hanging out in Camp 4. Through all the celebrations and bouldering, we noticed a group of young Brits. They were youngsters whose experience on English gritstone had made them confident on the toughest of routes and whose ears soon pricked up as we told of our experience on El Niño. Patch Hammond and Leo Houlding, barely eighteen years old, had taken the bait. They had no alpine experience or equipment but bucket loads of talent and energy. With their attitude of "big walling is easy!" they set off to tackle El Niño. They came across some classic problems when adopting big wall techniques but climbed all the better for it. Alternating the lead, the two were a powerful team. Houlding free climbed all pitches on sight bar two, either leading or seconding. On Black Dike and Missing Link he redpointed them on his second attempt. Also Hammond free climbed most of the route. Neither had any previous experience on the face … so theirs was a notable achievement and a pointer to the future.

Months later, the Tyrolean Much Mayer (with Richard Schipflinger), went up El Niño and topped out five days later. He redpointed the whole route. He did this with no prior research and did not spend any time prior to the ascent studying specific pitches. Even if he did not climb some of the pitches on-sight, he is still second only to Yuji Hirayama in successfully redpointing a route on his first attempt. It was now clear that the pioneer free climbers would not be alone on the big walls for very long. The way in which ascents come about is as varied as the spectrum of free climbers about today. There are redpoint ascents done in one or several days, free ascents lasting weeks or team-free-ascents where several climbers free climb a whole route as a group.

First free ascents naturally tend to follow the path of least resistance. In the summer of 2000, Tommy Caldwell and Beth Rodden worked on Lurking Fear (5.13c), a route which Steve Schneider had very nearly cracked a few years earlier. The difficulties they encountered and the July heat made it tough for the two of them. So they decided they would set up a free ascent by redpointing all the individual pitches, not in any particular order, but during several attempts over the span of twenty days. Caldwell and Nick Sagar used this same technique to successfully free climb Muir Wall (5.13c) one year later. Both routes demand extremely complex and problematic climbing that gives rise to this piecemeal approach. Thus, to clarify the style, both endeavours might be called, along with other similar examples of the genre, "hotchpotch" free ascents.

If one is on the look-out for further challenges, then you must ask when and who will redpoint these routes in one day? Lynn Hill managed it on The Nose in 1994, Thomas and I pulled it off in 1998 on the Free Rider. In 2002 Tommy Caldwell became the first person to make an individual redpoint ascent of the

Bunny
Slope

5.12c

5.12d

5.10a

Mammoth
Terraces

5.8

El Capitan

5.6

5.7

5.7

5.11a

Coffee
Corner

Beam
Flake

Half
Dollar

El Corazon

5.13a

5.11a

5.10c

5.12a

Fat City

5.10a

5.9

Beak
Flake

5.11a

5.10a

5.13b

Splitter
5.10b

5.11a

A5 - Traverse

5.12a

Kierke
gaard

5.11b

5.13a

5.12b

Chimney

5.9

Golden
Desert

5.10b

5.13a

5.10d

5.10c

5.11a

5.13b

5.8

Roof Traverse

5.10b

5.11a

5.10c

*The perfect hand-jamming crack of
the Splitter (5.10b), El Corazón, El Capitan*

*Pages 166 and 167: Rob Miller (belayed by
James Selvidge) on his route Quantum Mechanics
(5.13a), Washington Column*

Adrenaline! I am awake with the first light. I am lying on my back in my sleeping bag. Above me, the Beak Flake, a faint line which splits an otherwise featureless wall. The fine line of the flake stretches eighty metres starting ten metres above our bivouac ledge. There is an overhanging wave of compact granite between us and the flake – the toughest part of El Corazón. The two-millimetres-thick "steel" of an in-situ Bird Beak is the only protection here, hammered fifteen millimetres into the wall and eight metres above the ledge. There is a possibility that the steel will break under the shock of a fall and I have to realise that a fall could be serious. You can only consider taking such a risk if you can climb the following two metres in full control to remove all possibility of failure. This involves moving up the overhanging wall on side pulls and then making an all-out dyno to reach the Beak Flake.

The rope runs smoothly through the karabiner and a small sling ties it to the Bird Beak. Below, a very attentive Max belays me. Yet still I feel as if I am free soloing. I am scared but at the same time, know that I can do it. Controlling my fear before it turns to nervousness, I push on. Two side pulls, with footholds almost at the same height … I jump. Both hands off the face, my upper body arches its way up the wall, almost skimming the rock … speed … sights fixed … movements coordinated. My fingers grab the Beak Flake. I avert my eyes from my hands and look down the shadow of the flake. It is such a short part of this huge wall, but for me it encompasses everything I associate with climbing: athleticism, dynamism and precision.

Salathé Wall in a day (nineteen hours) in 2002. Even faster Yuji Hirayama (with Tamotsu Sugino) managed the same climb in a mere thirteen hours. All the rest of the free-climbed routes on El Capitan still lie in wait!*

There is however, another aspect to consider besides the pure technical climbing difficulties. Primarily a big wall is a playground of adventure, where climbing heads into the unknown. The less protection there is, the harder progress will be. Tension and fear are your companions, experience and self-confidence the keys to psychologically demanding and potentially dangerous routes. This game is about confronting and handling this danger, edging closer to the boundaries of the possible and calculating risks. It is a passionate game where muscle power is no more important than adrenaline levels.

Leo Houlding

30 THE PROPHET OF PURISM

When I arrived in September 2001, Yosemite no longer intimidated me as it had on my first visit in 1998 – in fact it was beginning to feel like home. I had spent six months there over five seasons and had been lucky enough to climb with many of the best Yosemite climbers during that time. From them I quickly learned the skills and techniques necessary for efficient movement on a big wall. El Capitan had transformed from the nightmarish wall I had seen in 1998 to the dream crag that I stood before now. Yosemite had become a playground. My imagination ran wild with the possibilities of what might be feasible by combining and building on what I had learned.

I wanted to do a new free route on El Capitan in the purest possible style. For me style is very important and something of an obsession. Searching for an ever-greater challenge and the quest for adventure inspires my climbing more than anything. This is why I am so against the use of bolts, particularly on El Capitan. Although I accept that on El Cap some may be necessary it is important that they are kept to an absolute minimum. First ascents are not about creating routes for other climbers to enjoy in safety and in the process make the first ascentionist famous. They are about a climber rising to the challenge of his chosen line, pushing himself to his limit in pursuit of the unknown and leaving the wall the way he discovered it, adventure intact for those who wish to follow. Exploration is the name of the game.

And if it is a game, then the use of bolts and prior inspection by aid or abseil is cheating. Why degrade the challenge? Surely there is more satisfaction to be gained in anything by tempting failure than in assuring success? I am convinced it is better to fail in superior style than to succeed in any other. I

believe for a two-man team to climb a new route on El Capitan, ground up, in a day, without a drill, sharing leads and seconding everything free is the ultimate challenge, the best possible style in which to climb El Capitan. Perhaps some would say that one climber should lead every pitch whilst the partner jumars. This is not my opinion.

My partner was Jason Pickles, a friend whom I'd gladly trust with my life. Our chosen line was built around Jay Smith's aid route Bad to the Bone. Being less than half the height of The Nose this area of wall provided a real possibility for a successful ascent in this style. Although it is only 500m high, this part of El Cap is renowned for run-out pitches on loose rock and is home to many of Yosemite's hardest aid routes.

Our first attempt came on 14 October 2001. We began climbing at 6.30 a.m. armed with two ropes, one 6mm haul line, a large but extremely lightweight free rack, a small haul rucksack containing a tiny selection of aid gear, three litres of water and a few energy bars. We made good progress over the initial but not particularly difficult pitches until I began to lead the fifth pitch. At that point the wall becomes much steeper and the rock quality deteriorates greatly. A complicated enigma of discontinuous cracks, bottomless dihedrals, flying arêtes and hanging roofs would have to be overcome to gain access to a big groove.

The climbing was of a standard and nature I have rarely experienced and never in such an environment. The rock is friable and delicate, the protection is sparse and difficult to arrange but the greatest anxiety is the route finding. The intricate nature of the rock constantly obscures the view of what is to come: endlessly examining the next section for holds, rests

Leo Houlding, belayed by Jason Pickles, on his uncompleted El Capitan climb – The Prophet

and gear; desperately trying to choose the correct passage through the unknown. Will I climb into a situation from which I cannot reverse? What if there is no protection up there?

Finally I committed to the groove on the left. I did the crux, a difficult rock-over in a position where a fall would almost certainly have had serious consequences. Continuing at a greatly reduced pace I eventually stumbled across the old bolt belay from the aid route. Jason followed. He too felt the pitch to be of an exceptionally severe nature. Although it was merely a warm-up for what came next – the Screamer pitch.

By now we were deeply involved in the route. More of the same delicate sandy rock led up a flying corner to a small roof. From a wide stem I examined the continuation of the dihedral. It did not look possible. After a short while I noticed the scar left by a copperhead underneath the roof, a couple of metres to my left. An unlikely foot traverse on invisible edges, grasping the sloping lip of the roof with my hands, led to a reasonable foothold protruding from a hanging arête. Adrift in a vertical ocean, I balanced on the acute foothold in an incredibly exposed position. Above me was an inspiring and terrifying sight – the section of climbing that was to be the most demanding I have ever done.

The rock had changed to a more solid but still flaky, golden granite. About twenty metres higher I could see a selection of bolts and old tat forming a belay. One of the lead ropes was clipped to a micro wire by my foot on the left side of the arête. The haul line hung free all the way down to Jason at the belay thirty metres below. The other lead rope came horizontally to my harness from the right. Some six metres up and to my left there was an old bolt. The

Left: Leo Houlding on his boulder problem, Wizard

crux of the pitch proved to be the move to get to it. A desperate sideways press off a small incut side-pull to a distant flat edge. I did the move but was too drained to contemplate more scary climbing so I clipped the dangerously rusted bolt with a shock absorbing quick draw (or screamer) and rested on it. It held. Tiny but positive edges led, without protection, up a vague groove in a gently leaning wall to another bolt in a blank area of rock about ten metres higher. I could not tell if it would be possible to clip this. Summoning the courage and determination to continue pushed me to my limit.

A more perfectly horrendous test of climbing ability and nerve I cannot imagine. Every move presented a torturous decision whether or not to run it out further. Just as the relief that it's too hard to continue starts to take grip, another good foothold appears. A positive edge invites another move. Just one more move? At the limit of my reach, with the karabiner held by the tips of my fingers I managed to clip another screamer into the next bolt and hang on it. By now I was utterly exhausted but had come too far to be defeated. The next move confirmed my suspicion that this pitch was a masterpiece, meant to be climbed. A full body length mantelshelf on to a small incut ledge on an overhanging wall followed. Had the ledge been a few centimetres smaller or the hold a few centimetres further away I could not have done it. More big moves on small edges, way above the dubious bolt led by a hairline crack to a final section of easier climbing and the belay. It is amazing that it went free. Unknowingly Jay Smith had placed just enough bolts to make it possible, though still exceptionally bold. If they had not been there I would not have attempted to free the pitch.

By now it was 4 o'clock. As we are only half-way up the wall it was too late to continue. We retreated

leaving no rope fixed. Tragically on our next attempt Jason fell on the first pitch injuring his hip quite badly. I had two more attempts with different partners re-climbing the whole route each time. Hoping to reach the high point more quickly and with more ease, leaving enough time and energy for an assault on the upper half of the wall. Ultimately I only added one pitch but managed to climb everything to that point without falling.

If we had attempted the climb in a more conventional style we may have succeeded in making a new free route on El Capitan. However attempting the route ground up, climbing into uncharted terrain without any previous exploration was a more powerful and rewarding experience than any other piece of climbing I have ever done. The fear, desire, concentration and fulfillment I felt pushing so hard were extraordinary. To make that next move, to push yourself further into the unknown, further from safety, committing more and more to your own ability, judgement and belief.

This style of ascent adds a new dimension to free climbing. It demands advanced skills – not only those of climbing, but much more fundamental powers of self-confidence and overcoming fear. It is satisfying on a much deeper, more profound level. If we had aided or rappelled the route first, this pitch would have been a completely different experience. Nowhere near as hard or memorable. As climbing continues to evolve, old techniques will be replaced by new and today's test pieces will be tomorrow's trade routes. Climbing on El Cap is always going to be incredible but for those who are willing to push the limits, to try to do more with less, the rewards will always be greatest. Whether the route is completed or not.

Left and right. Leo Houlding, prior to and taking off on his rope jump from the summit of El Capitan

Mark Chapman

31 Outro

I am no longer the young awestruck boy who first experienced Yosemite all those years ago. Though my passion for climbing remains, my life has changed much, as has Yosemite climbing. The seemingly impossible has been climbed, sport routes coexist with traditional ones and Camp 4 has become a second home to the international climbing community. It seems at times that English is the foreign language. They come to climb, to live out a dream, and just perhaps, if they are lucky experience a bit of magic from an earlier time. For me, as I drive around the Valley floor, or wander through Camp 4, traces of that magic linger everywhere. When it casts its spell my mind travels back in time, down the long road that has brought Yosemite and me together. I am reminded of climbs, of good times and bad, of friends that now walk with me only in my memories. As I close my eyes to the past, I cannot help but wonder what the future holds.

The Valley meadows by the Merced in the fall

CLIMBING STYLES

FREE CLIMBING Moving up rock using only one's own body and the natural characteristics of the cliff (holds, cracks, slots etc). The rope and equipment are used only for protection.

FREE ASCENT The complete route is climbed without using aid of any kind by one person. This is ideally done on sight but can also be claimed if done by redpoint or pink point.

REDPOINT A continuous free ascent of any previously attempted or practised route/rope length (pitch). This will involve placing protection equipment as one proceeds.

PINK POINT A free ascent where the runners have been pre-placed, after practice the rope is pulled down and the runners are then clipped during the ascent.

FLASH A free ascent of a route on first attempt using information about the route by watching other climbers do the route or inquiring from others who know the route.

ON SIGHT A free ascent of a route on first attempt, sight unseen, and without gathering information (other than the normal guidebook description) from others who know the route.

FREE SOLO A free ascent without using ropes or protection.

SOLO Climbing alone but with periodic (or total) protection of a back-rope, and protection points, or even by aid climbing.

AID CLIMBING (aka Techno Climbing) Making progress on a climb using artificial aid. This generally involves using tape etriers or slings attached to fixed or placed pitons, bolts, bat hooks, RPs, nuts, bashies and camming devices. Pendulums or tension traverses may be used. Easy aid-climbing might involve dynamic pulling on karabiners clipped to insitu pitons or bolts. Hard aid climbing (on featureless rock with shallow cracks, seams and edges, or on sections of friable, insecure rock) relies on very marginal forms of support. A fall might result in stripping many points of aid. Such falls are often long and potentially serious but in some cases (close to the ground or above large ledges) can be *very* serious.

FREE CLIMBING ON BIG WALLS
(Note: Most parties still climb Yosemite big walls with a mix of free and aid)

REDPOINT ASCENT – each rope length must be climbed redpoint. If the redpoint ascent is claimed by two climbers who rotate the lead, the leader must climb the respective ropelength redpoint, while the other must follwo the same rope length free as well.

INDIVIDUAL REDPOINT – one climber leads all the pitches free while the other follows by any convenient manner.

FREE ASCENT – All rope lengths of a big wall are climbed by one climber ideally redpoint but some of them, less satisfactorily, done pink point of free while following. This is ideally done in the process of a continuous ascent but there is now a growing trend to claim free ascents done in "hotchpotch" manner.

TEAM FREE ASCENT – The ascent in a team, where every pitch is climbed free by one member, while the rest follow in the most expeditious manner possible.

Editor's Note: Redpointing and its variations generally apply to routes/pitches of extreme technical difficulty or sustained strenuosity, that (currently) require some sort of pre-practice or pre-knowledge to be able to make a free ascent. The normal style on easier climbs (at least up to 5.11 6a) is to make an ascent without pre-practice which is considered poor style, often inconvenient to others, and ideally avoided. On such climbs (selected to match the team's ability), the conventional approach would be for the party to aim to achieve a competent, speedy and trouble-free ascent.

Yosemite	U.K.	UIAA	France
5.10a	E1 5a/b	VI+	6a
5.10b	E1 5b	VII-	6a+
5.10c	E2 5b	VII	6b
5.10d	E3 5b		6b+
5.11a	E3 5c	VII+	6c
5.11b	E3 5c	VIII-	6c+
5.11c	E4 5c		7a
5.11d	E4 6a	VIII	7a+
5.12a	E5 6a	VIII+	7b
5.12b	E5 6a	IX-	7b+
5.12c	E5 6b		7c
5.12d	E6 6b	IX	7c+
5.13a	E6 6b	IX+	8a
5.13b	E7 6c	X-	
5.13c	E7 6c		8a+
5.13d	E7 6c	X	8b
5.14a	E8 7a	X+	8b+
5.14b	E8 7a		8c

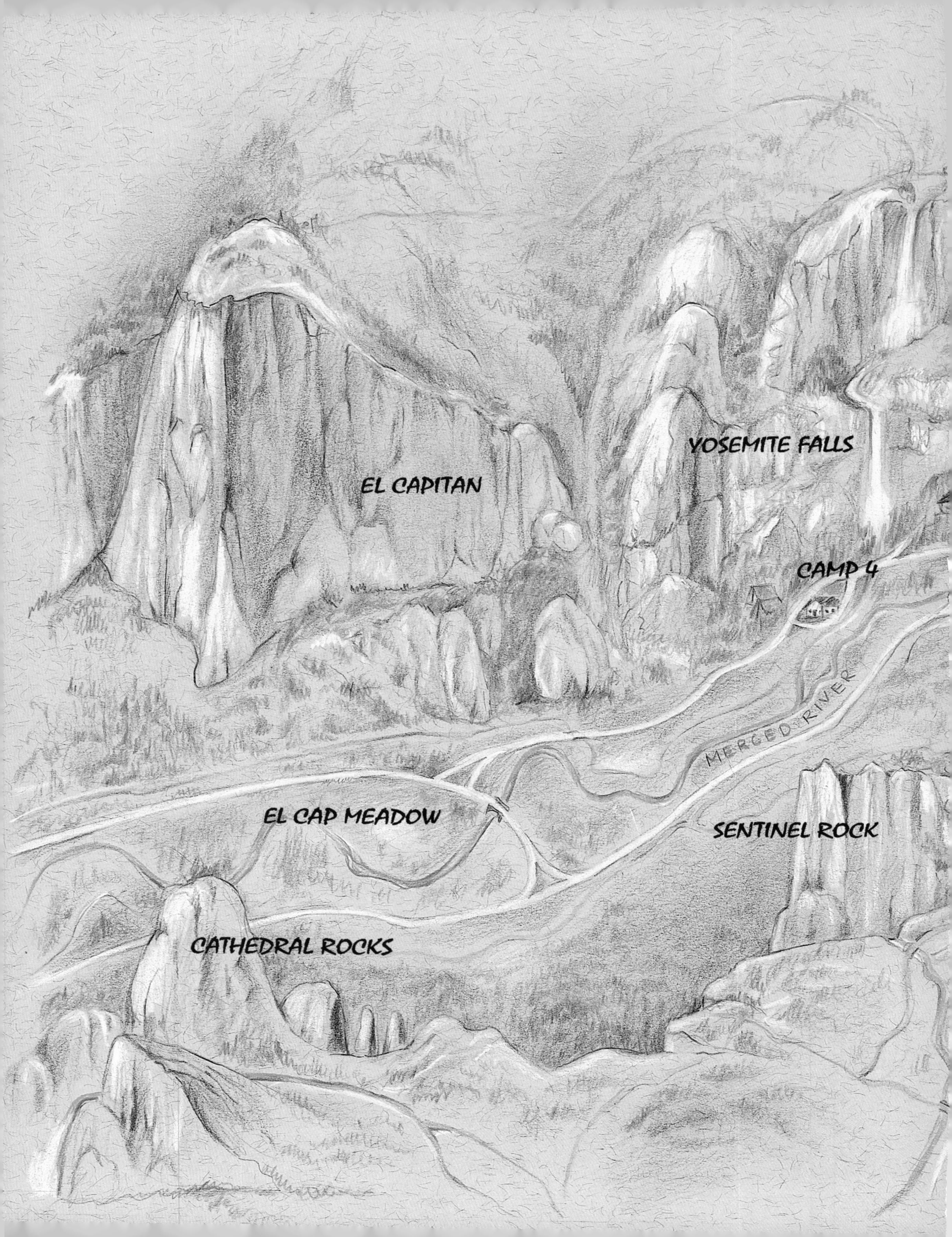

EL CAPITAN

YOSEMITE FALLS

CAMP 4

MERCED RIVER

EL CAP MEADOW

SENTINEL ROCK

CATHEDRAL ROCKS